IVAN ZHAVORONKOV

# Nietzsche's Philosophy: Translation and Interpretation

A Collection of Articles

Edited by John Woodsworth

York University
Toronto, 2012

Nietzsche's Philosophy:
Translation and Interpretation. *Toronto 2012.*
A collection of articles. York University.
Edited by John Woodsworth
*Copyright © 2011 by Ivan Zhavoronkov.*
*All rights reserved.* No part of this book may be used
or reproduced in any manner whatsoever
without written permission.

*For more information on edition or to place an order,
please email at:* zarathustra2001us@yahoo.com

ISBN: 978-0-9737762-2-5

Nietzsche's Philosophy:
Translation and Interpretation. 105 pages
Page format: 5.25" x 8"
Cover Design by Ivan Zhavoronkov
2012•Published by York University

Published by York University in Toronto.
Printed in the USA.

# CONTENTS

## Symbolism in Friedrich Nietzsche's *Thus Spake Zarathustra*
(2009)

1. Introduction..................................................................5
2. Definition of the Symbol................................................6
3. Earth Symbols of the Overman.....................................9
4. Conclusion..................................................................15
5. Works Cited................................................................16

## The Evolution of Nietzsche's *Übermensch* in *ALSO SPRACH ZARATHUSTRA* Through Translation
(2008)

1. Introduction................................................................17
2. The Phenomenon of the *Übermensch*........................19
3. Translators' Backgrounds............................................26
4. Translation as Interpretation........................................30
5. *Übermensch* as Superman, Overman and Overhuman.35
6. Conclusion..................................................................45
7. Works Cited................................................................46

## Nietzsche: Translation as Perspectivism
(2010)

1. Introduction..................................................48
2. The Truth of Reality and Translation................49
3. What is a Healthy Translation?........................57
4. Translation as Self-Conquest..........................61
5. Conclusion....................................................69
6. Works Cited..................................................70

## Nietzsche's Interpretation of the Bible
(2009)

1. Introduction..................................................71
2. Judaism vs. Christianity.................................72
3. Nietzsche contra Paul....................................78
4. Conclusion....................................................90
5. Works Cited..................................................91

## Love of Neighbour in Nietzsche's Philosophy
(2010)

1. Introduction..................................................93
2. Christ, the Overman, Eternal Return................94
3. Conclusion..................................................102
4. Works Cited................................................103

# Symbolism in Friedrich Nietzsche's *Thus Spake Zarathustra* (2008)

## Introduction

Friedrich Nietzsche's *Thus Spake Zarathustra* is a valuable contribution not only to contemporary philosophy, but also philology. One of the literary devices that Nietzsche employs throughout his masterpiece is the symbol. It is precisely by using literary symbols, not mere signs — as some scholars of Nietzsche's language such as Stegmaier and Marsden think — that the author expresses his philosophical ideas in *Thus Spake Zarathustra*.

Nietzsche deconstructs traditional (ancient, biblical) symbols and creates his own set of symbols to structure his existentialist thought. I contend that Nietzsche's thought and symbol merge together and make us readers confront our traditional, symbolic understanding of the world and become questionable to ourselves as creative human beings, as creators of our own world. The purpose of this research is to unfold the nature of this confrontation.

## 2. Definition of the Symbol

Etymologically the term symbol means a token, a sign.[1] The symbol is an object which represents something. It has a significance, a concept. Symbolist poets, such as Eliot, Mallarmé, Baudelaire and others view the symbol as a poetic image. Nietzsche is a poet and uses literary images, but that does not immediately guarantee that his images are symbols. His symbols must be proven signifiable.

According to Ferdinand de Saussure,[2] each sign is an arbitrary union of signifier and signified. In this respect, Nietzsche's literary images are signs inasmuch as they represent something. S. S. Averintsev defines the symbol as "an image taken in the aspect of its signification, and a sign vested with all the organic and inexhaustible multiplicity of meanings of an image." (Averintsev 607) Yet, according to Derrida, a text carries "a plurality of significance" (Cuddon 210) to the point of having no meaning. In Nietzsche's case, the symbol of the Overman readily invokes the symbol of his herald, Zarathustra, and the doctrine of will to power and eternal return, which in turn have their own symbols, e.g., the serpent and eagle as symbols of eternal recurrence. Our task is to find meaning in Nietzsche's symbols not by combating but by tapping into them.

---

[1] The term symbol "derives from the Greek verb *symbollein*, 'to throw together,' and its noun *symbolon*, a 'mark', 'emblem', 'token' or 'sign,' " according to *The Dictionary of Literary Terms and Literary Theory* by John Anthony Cuddon, (884–885).
[2] See *Cours de linguistique générale*.

According to Stegmaier and Marsden, Zarathustra uses signs to communicate his doctrines. However, these "signs" are literary symbols, for they are wrapped in vague poetic imagery perceived not as much by reason as by heartfelt emotions. The admixture of poeticism in the sign-composition of the world makes all reality *as if real* through ephemeral literary symbols that Nietzsche employs to show that the whole existence is made up of floating ghostly apparitions – symbols – that the human being himself creates for himself to feel himself comfortable in his self-fashioned, fluctuant, undulating environment. For Nietzsche, the emotive aspect of the sign is intricately bound up with a profound poetic image and expresses ultimate sensuous ambiguity and various unique experiences thereof.

When Nietzsche realised that it is human nature to read meaning into the meaninglessness of reality, he recognised Christianity as a mere system of symbols. His next move was to confront biblical symbols and challenge all other socio-historical symbols by recreating them and creating his own symbols to create uncommon, uncomfortable experiences in the consciousness of the reader accustomed and attuned to traditional symbolism, to take the reader's mind off from stupefying traditionalism, to awaken, in Anatoly Nazirov's terms, "people unawakened from their sleep."[3]

---

[3] A quotation from Anatoly Nazirov's philosophical *poema Zarathustra* (1993), p. 47, inspired by F. Nietzsche's *Thus Spake Zarathustra*, translated by Ivan Zhavoronkov. Toronto: York University, 2011.

The reader is called upon not only to tear mentally away from traditional symbolism but also to stand the challenges of new, multiple symbolism: to immerse himself in the ocean of Nietzsche's symbols — not to drown but to emerge refreshed, thus overcoming his own customary worldview. The coherent meaning is to be found in overcoming the ever-new billowing waves of Nietzsche's tempestuous ocean of symbolism by going under and so over them and oneself, just as overcoming the untoward adversities of life by accepting them, affirming them and thus enhancing our life.

At the base of Nietzsche's symbols there lies a poetic image that has a profound, philosophical meaning. *Eidos* becomes *logos* with Socrates which metamorphoses back into *eidos* with Nietzsche – yet purged from mythological, religious and moral blemishes. And it is a new kind of *eidos* – an *eidos-logos* type, Nietzsche's type, from which emanate art, thinking and science. Nietzsche's *eidos* symbols also admit of a new *logos* to express both a poetical image and philosophical thought. The *eidos-logos* symbols of Nietzsche combine some abstract philosophical notions such as being, will and becoming with symbolic images, which determines the literary, imagerial character of his fundamentally philosophical work. Thought and symbol merge together to confront traditional symbolism. The criterion of cultural determinativeness is useful in symbol identification and in researching the change from traditional (biblical) to new, personal symbolism in Nietzsche's text.

## 3. Earth Symbols of the Overman

In "The Symbolism and Celebration of the Earth in Nietzsche's *Zarathustra,*" Weiss discusses the symbolism of the earth and the shattering of onto-theological tradition in Nietzsche's text but provides no direct links to the symbolism of the Last Man, Zarathustra and the Overman. Nietzsche's all-encompassing symbol is the Overman, and the Earth is one of his symbols. The earth symbols of the Overman are Zarathustra's symbols of his return home. But what does it mean for Zarathustra to return *home*? Zarathustra's return home is his return to himself, his mind, his thinking, his thought by affirming his own life.

Before Zarathustra returns home, he is constantly followed by his own shadow, the last man, till it finally vanishes at the hour of noon, and his animals – the eagle and the serpent – appear to signal the necessity of his returning home, for they appear when Zarathustra begins to feel most lonely. Upon returning home, he inevitably falls into lonesomeness. Zarathustra returns from humans into his cave, where he enjoys his spirit in solitude and nourishes his soul through thinking. The appearance of the animals, the disappearance of the shadow and the return home are Zarathustra's moment of becoming an Overman. The Overman is the meaning of the Earth, and the Earth is the symbol of home for the Overman. Finally, Zarathustra's return home is humanity coming back to its instinctive, corporeal nature and becoming divine through life-affirming creativity. This is achieved when the Earth, the home of the Overman, is illumined by the brightest light of day at noon.

Zarathustra's shadow represents a wanderer, the last man, who is looking for a home – the home of the Overman – who thus desires his homecoming, his coming into his own home, coming to his own self.[4] In this coming to itself, the shadow overcomes its alienation and becomes one with man at the hour of noon, and disappears as such. Twelve o'clock is Zarathustra's symbol of the Great Noontide, "the hour of the coming of the *Übermensch*" (Grillaert 55), which is a symbol of the Overman himself. The becoming one, man's becoming what he *is*, the becoming as the overcoming of man so far, as his coming into the being of Overman, is a moment of both man's and his shadow's repose upon the Earth after long wanderings within the labyrinth of existence. Thus man finds his rest in the Overman. When Zarathustra returns home, he resurrects the Overman in himself. The Nietzschean resurrection is the resurrection of a healthy body which speaks of the meaning of the Earth, not of the world beyond. The last man is the deceased animal stuck between reality and the beyond, whereas the Overman is perfectly healthy on Earth.

Zarathustra's home is on top of a mountain. The height of the mountain represents the transcendence of the last man by man himself on his path upward to the heavenly Overman. The height symbolises the exaltation of human aspiration to what is most sublime and divine[5] in human nature. The cave at this height of the mountain, at which

---

[4] Zarathustra's true self is the meaning of the Earth.
[5] Only the life-negating God is dead; whereas the life-affirming divinity is alive for Nietzsche.

Zarathustra finds himself when most lonely and thoughtful, is "the symbol of the bowels of the earth," the womb of the Earth "which will give birth to the Overman" (Weiss 39) – the symbol of the Earth, out of whose bowels' profundity the deepest thoughtfulness of human existence arises in the appearance of the Overman. Thus, the highest and lowest points of the Earth, symbolising the deepest thought and sublimation which man attains by creative thinking, embrace all realms of human existence. In this respect the mountain and the cave become man's works wrought beyond good and evil, God and devil, that point away from the present man to a man of the future, the Overman.

In the Bible, however, Jesus is not alone: he preaches a sermon to his disciples on the mountain. Zarathustra is all alone. Furthermore, the resurrection of Jesus Christ is symbolic of his ascent to the heavenly, spiritual world as opposed to the earthly, material, carnal world. The Nietzschean resurrection is somewhat different in nature: Zarathustra, while dwelling in the cave, immersed in abysmal thought, cares for his body, passions and desires; they make him feel himself alive, for they have life-forces that drive him toward the height of creative imagination and action. Earth and heaven are blended together within him. Thus Nietzsche rethinks and deconstructs the biblical symbol of resurrection into both the spiritual and corporeal conception of the Overman.

Zarathustra is an advocate of life on earth, between heaven and hell. The earth is an all-inclusive symbol of inner relationships between chaos and cosmos, creation and destruction, good and evil, the sacred and the secular. Earth symbolism is thus ambivalent by nature. We find the underworld in Greek mythology, where the dead and the living, in their afterlife, are punished according to their actions in their previous, earthly life. This idea of punishment is akin to the Christian idea of hell as opposed to the Kingdom of Heaven. None of these constitutes Zarathustra's pure vision of the world: what is down below represents the deepest thought; what is up high symbolises the sublimation of the most profound ideas. The going upward from the deep below is the life force of the will to power. In Nietzsche's *Thus Spake Zarathustra* the Earth may be understood to symbolise the chaotic system of the will to power, the foundation of Nietzsche's ontogeny, i.e., growth of being, which emanates from the deepest and heaviest burden of thought down below to the most aerial lightness of the exalted spirit up high. That is the direction in which the energy of the will to power flows, earth in heaven and heaven in earth.

Zarathustra's animals are the eagle and the serpent. They appear when Zarathustra thinks his most abysmal thought: eternal recurrence as will willing itself. There are three aspects of these animals – the physical, the character and the sensuous – which Heidegger suggests in his *Nietzsche* but does not envision as fundamentally symbolic, let alone as manifestations of shattered traditional symbols. The **physical aspect** of the animals' original symbolic representation consists in the eagle's soaring in circles high up in heaven and the serpent's coiling around the eagle's neck – both represent the eternal recurrence of the same. The **character aspect** of the animals' both original (Nietzschean) and traditional symbolic representation consists in the eagle's being the proudest animal and thus representing the pride and exaltation of the superman, and in the serpent being wise and hence representing the wisdom and discernment of the superman. The **sensuous aspect** of the animals' original symbolism consists of both animals appearing when Zarathustra is alone and lonely. Thus they represent "the loneliest loneliness" of Zarathustra. (Heidegger *Nietzsche* 47) All three aspects are conjoined in a profoundly **sensuous imagery** symbolic of the essence of Zarathustra as the teacher of eternal return unfolded in the nature of the superman. This sensuous symbolic imagery is in its essence *poetic* and as such serves the purpose of expressing the philosophical ideas of the superman: will to power and eternal return.

The Nietzschean serpent and eagle, wisdom and pride, do not find their full equivalents in the Biblical ones. In the Old Testament, for example, in the story of Adam and Eve, the serpent that has cheated Eve into eating of the tree of knowledge of good and evil, symbolises (sexual) instinct rather than wisdom as it does in Nietzsche's context. Pride in Christianity is not a virtue either. Also, the Nietzschean serpent is different from the Greek one. As is known, the serpent in the cult of Asclepius in ancient Greece, god of medicine and healing, was identified with health. The snake could also be a sexual symbol; for example, in myth we find Zeus impregnating Persephone in the form of a snake. This is especially conveyed through the double symbolism of the Sabazius ritual: "snake for phallus, artifact for snake," where the initiand dreads sexual associations as if he or she were about to touch a snake, being unable to tell the live creature from the artifact in the light of the torches. (Burkert 106)

Although traditionally the serpent has been identified with shrewdness and cunningness (and sin), which has some hints at keenness and perspicacity, the serpent in *Thus Spake Zarathustra* symbolises wisdom only on one condition: when there is the eagle of pride present. In other words, the sublimation of wisdom with the help of the soaring eagle of pride is necessary for wisdom to reign above all, whereas, on the other hand, if only pride remains, wisdom is immediately replaced by folly. For the purpose of keeping the two together, there is an implication in Nietzsche's context that the serpent and the eagle are inseparable from each other: the serpent, not as an enemy but as a friend, is coiled around the eagle's neck. This coiling around is the fusion of the serpent of wisdom with the eagle of pride, which symbolises the eternal return of the creative will to power toward self-realisation.

As to the eagle, it is a proud animal and is traditionally associated with conquest and power (this probably comes from the hunting qualities of the bird), which is characteristic of the Roman Empire. The statue of the emperor Claudius in the guise of Jupiter, for example, shows an eagle at the feet of the emperor looking up at him, symbolising his supreme power and control.

As is shown above, Nietzsche's eagle and serpent are not totally historical, traditional symbols but are strongly coloured by his conception of existence and the world as the will to power and eternal return. Thus by using traditional symbolism in his *Thus Spake Zarathustra* and by rethinking and reworking it to the point of self-transcendence to serve the purpose of expressing philosophical ideas about Being as the will to power unfolded in the eternal recurrent becoming, Nietzsche deconstructs, with all the might of two-and-a-half-thousand years of cultural heritage, the innermost core of traditional symbolism itself and, in so doing, lays an unshakeable foundation for the revaluation of all prior values.

## Conclusion

Nietzsche invented and used his own unique symbols to demonstrate not only the power of thought, *logos*, but also the power of the word, *eidos*. Thinking as saying and saying as thinking are merged together in his symbols. I would like to conclude by saying that if we have in the meantime, while considering Nietzsche's symbolism, become questionable to ourselves as unique creative human beings, it is likely that it is a sign, or possibly a symbol, of our proximity to ourselves in the realm of transition from a traditional symbolic worldview to new, unbound and unbounded symbolic interpretations of our own view of our own world.

## Works Cited

Averintsev S. S. "Simvol" *Filosofskiy entsiklope-dicheskiy slovar* [*Philosophical Encyclopedic Dictionary*], Moscow: Sovetskaya entsiklopediya, 1983.
Burkert, Walter *Ancient Mystery Cults*, Cambridge, MA: Harvard University Press, 1987.
Cuddon, John Anthony *Dictionary of Literary Terms and Literary Theory*, London: Penguin Books, 1999.
Grillaert, Nel "Determining One's Fate: A Delineation of Nietzsche's Conception of Free Will." *The Journal of Nietzsche Studies* (#31, 2006): 42-60.
Heidegger M. *Nietzsche* ed. & tr. David Farrell Krell, HarperSanFrancisco *A division of* Harper Collins Publishers: 1991, Vol. 4, p. 6.
Nazirov A. E. *Zarathustra* (po motivam proizvedeniya F. Nietzsche "Tak govoril Zarathustra") Filosofskaya poema [inspired by F. Nietzsche's *Thus Spake Zarathustra*; Philosophical Poema], St.Petersburg: Tekhpribor, 1993. Trans. Ivan Zhavoronkov. Toronto: York University, 2011.
Weiss, Allen S. "The Symbolism and Celebration of the Earth in Nietzsche's 'Zarathustra.'" *SubStance* 8.1 (#22, 1979): 39-47.

# The Evolution of Nietzsche's *Übermensch* in *ALSO SPRACH ZARATHUSTRA* Through Translation
(2008)

## Introduction

The following research is aimed at tracing the development of the notion of Nietzsche's *Übermensch* in his *Also sprach Zarathustra* through the medium of translation. Three particular English translations, namely Thomas Common's, Walter Kaufmann's and Graham Parkes', will be looked at. The Thomas Common translation is the earliest of the three and dates from the end of the nineteenth and the beginning of the twentieth centuries. The Walter Kaufmann translation comes to us from the 1960s. And the Graham Parkes translation appears with the dawn of the 21$^{st}$ century. This selection reflects the three different translations of the word *Übermensch* by translators coming from different backgrounds, namely *Superman, Overman* and *Overhuman*. The focus of the research will be *Zarathustra's Prologue*, for it is the opening gateway into the world of Nietzsche's work. Nietzsche's ideas are contained and expressed in the prologue — literally on the first page — in their entirety.

Another reason for this choice is that these translations were made at different times, namely, starting from the influence of poetical classicism echoing from the 18$^{th}$ century (e.g. Goethe in Germany) and emerging nihilism (of Christian values), the rise of new philosophical values

(Nietzschean existentialism) in the 19th century, to be fully appreciated at the early middle of the 20th century (Heidegger), with the death of God regarded as the death of metaphysics with the subsequent scientific boom (according to Nietzsche humanity kills God; by killing God, Heidegger adds, humanity kills itself (e.g. the creation of the atom bomb; "the wasteland grows"[6])).

The focus will be on Nietzsche's term *Übermensch*. The phenomenon of the *Übermensch* will be explicated by unearthing its historical emergence against the background of nineteenth-century nihilism. For this purpose Martin Heidegger's analysis, as well as Andrei Bely's interpretation of the image of Nietzsche's *Übermensch*, will be used to reinterpret this term as the revaluation of all values, the will to power, and the eternal return.

The essence of translation will also be expounded upon and will parallel the understanding of the *Übermensch* in light of its translational transformation — to reinterpret the *Übermensch* as a synthesis of art, philosophy and science, while also taking a comparative approach to the translations of *Übermensch* as *Superman, Overman* and *Overhuman*. It will be seen that Common translates the *Übermensch* poetically, that Kaufmann's translation elicits the philosophical traits of the *Übermensch*, while Parkes equivalently translates it linguistically. Translation variants will also be offered for *Übermensch* to take a broader view

---

[6] This phrase from Nietzsche's *Also sprach Zarathustra* is given significant attention by Heidegger who shows — in *What is Called Thinking?* — that science does not think (the way thinkers think).

of the principal translation difficulty encountered by the translators.

For the purpose of comparing the three different translations of Nietzsche's *Übermensch*, it will be necessary first to consider the importance of *Übermensch*, its significance, its image and the role it plays in the work.

## 2. The Phenomenon of the *Übermensch*

For the 20$^{th}$-century philosopher Martin Heidegger, the question of Being became the question of Western philosophy. According to his interpretation, Nietzsche's *Übermensch* springs from *nihilism* at the end of the nineteenth century. Nihilism is the negation of prior values, the death of the Christian God, the *transcendent*, the truth of being as a whole, the end of metaphysics. It ends itself in that it fulfils itself. Nihilism fulfils, perfects itself, and its ending in the history of Western metaphysics is the beginning of a *new* valuation of prior values — in Nietzsche's words, "revaluation of all values hitherto."[7] Thus, "the revaluation thinks Being for the first time as value," says Heidegger. (Heidegger: 4: 6)

The uprooting of the *need* for prior values in their place in the transcendent stems from the "growing ignorance of past values." "Revaluation of prior values" is primarily "the metamorphosis of all valuation heretofore" and breeds "a new need for values." (Heidegger: 4: 6) There must be a

---

[7] David Farrell Krell's translation of *Nietzsche* by Heidegger, HarperSanFrancisco *A division of* Harper Collins *Publishers*: 1991, vol. 4, p. 6

new basis for the revaluation of all values, which is a new interpretation of beings as a whole. The interpretation issues not from a transcendent but from beings themselves. Nietzsche defines the basic character of being as a/the will to power, that is, power accruing power for its own *overpowering*. Only power posits, validates and decides values.

All being as incessant self-overpowering is a continual becoming "in the cyclical increase of power" and therefore always keeps recurring. Being as will to power is a recurring, self-overpowering becoming and hence is also defined as "the eternal recurrence of the same" (as will willing itself). The "will to power" tells *what* beings are in their "essence" and "the eternal recurrence of the same" tells *how* beings of such an essence must be in their entirety. (Heidegger: 4: 7, 8) More philosophically put, the will to power is the *essentia* of beings and the eternal recurrence of the same is their *existentia*.

Classical nihilism takes man beyond himself to the *Übermensch*, who is the supreme, absolute, purest will to power, the one and only value, the meaning of the "earth," "the singular form of human existence" in which every man participates, "a true being, close to "reality" and "life." (Heidegger 4: 9) Thus, Nietzsche thinks the essence of *nihilism* in the direction of world history in the context of the "revaluation of all values," the "will to power," the "eternal recurrence of the same," and the "Overman."

The conception of the *Übermensch* is deeply rooted in ancient philosophy. The Nietzschean conception of the *Übermensch* is atheistic. It boldly proclaims that *"God is dead!"* Now with God dead, man remains alone, to be superior to the decomposing God. The *Übermensch* is the highest phase of man that man himself has ever known. The *Übermensch* is man's sole orientation in life.

Nietzsche's *Übermensch* is born of Nietzsche's view of the human being to replace the biblical (and other gods) God who died when nihilism reached its peak, with values collapsing on themselves: nothing of the real world is true; everything is permitted.

In *Also sprach Zarathustra,* Nietzsche creates both a poetic and philosophical image of the *Übermensch*. It is an image of a man that overcomes himself and the present-day world by transcending all morality, for man does not know what is good or what is evil for himself.

*Übermensch* has also been interpreted as a man of the future that has rid himself of all the present-day falsities in thinking. It is the cult of a strong personality driven by the will to power. According to Nietzsche, the will to power is an interpretation of man's activity. The forces of human instincts spur man into creativity. The will to power is an interpretation of both the human nature and the world that humans create.

The death of God proclaimed by Nietzsche stems from the death of man, who, experiencing the decline of his 'faith' in the old (Christian) values, negates the real world and thus abolishes also the apparent world ('the world beyond,' 'eternal life,' 'redemption,' 'good and evil,' 'truth,' 'the Father in Heaven,' etc.). The old Christian values with which the whole of the Western philosophy was permeated finally devaluate and fall short of themselves, and now man needs to create new values.

Nietzsche revisits morality thus: "He that falls, let him fall" to echo evangelic morality: "Let the dead bury their dead."[8] Nietzsche is thus protesting against the weaklings' taking over the strong, against everyday life full of vice and lies. Nietzsche's *Übermensch* is a poetic image, vague in its meaning. It is the apophasis, that is, the negation of the image of man, of the common man, the man of the herd, "the last man."[9] Such negation implies superiority over life's worthlessness.

Humanity has been unconscious of its own creative, *wilful* development through history. Nietzsche was the first to note that all that humanity had created so far was a manifestation not of its will to truth, as had been believed by prior (moral) philosophers (e.g. Kant), but of its will to power. Nietzsche further suggests that it is time to continue to create but consciously, while aspiring to the goal that can never be attained because life, existence, is deep, unfathomable, and eternal in every Now. Thus Nietzsche affirms life.

As Andrei Bely interprets Nietzsche's conception of a human being: the more unsure the will is of the purpose of its own development, the more readily it becomes a creative instinct. (Bely: e-text "Friedrich Nietzsche") The primary instinct of self-preservation is only the basic constituent of the human nature, which soon reaches its boundary, its limit. This boundary or limit is a new kind of humankind. The *Übermensch* is an all-encompassing

---

[8] Matth. 8: 22.
[9] I Cor. 15:45.

literary image of this kind: it is dictated by the creative will of a day-dreaming human being.

The dream of creativity is in conflict with the reality of nihilism it confronts. The dream of the *Übermensch* comes closer to reality for Nietzsche than that reality does to itself. The *Übermensch* is *the* man who overcomes his sufferance by creating things anew. Sufferance is conducive to self-overcoming. Nietzsche uses the teleological image of the *Übermensch* to preach man's sufferance caused by life's instinct, thus affirming life as self-conscious creativity in man's constant striving for power through self-realisation.

Nietzsche does not touch upon the traits of an absolutely free individual. However, he represents them through the *Übermensch*. Nietzsche paraphrases Kant here and defines the categorical imperative as an aspiration to creative freedom, thereby proclaiming a new morality for humanity, that of conscious creativity.

The poetic image of the *Übermensch* in *Also sprach Zarathustra* presents a certain translation difficulty due to its phonemic, morphological and semantic structure, and finally because it is simply a neologism of Nietzsche's, central to his work and to understanding of human beings. Besides, the *Übermensch* is also a complex literary image overloaded with philosophical thinking.

Nietzsche was the first to recognise the danger and the necessity of a change in the realm of essential thinking, the moment in history when humankind was about to assume dominion of the earth as a whole, as Heidegger explains, adding that the human is a rational animal, meaning the human is both a sensual (physical, i.e., his body) suprasensual (reasoning or beyond the physical or supraphysical, i.e., metaphysical) being. Man, being as such, is "the as yet (unconceived) undetermined animal," according to Nietzsche. For his nature to be determined, man must be "carried beyond himself" (Heidegger: 58), Heidegger thus interprets Nietzsche, who calls man "the last man" — in the sense that he is unable to rise above himself to do what is essentially right because he has not attained his own full development. Man's nature harbours the passage from the physical to the supra-physical. And the bridge to the nature of *Übermensch* is man's own self-overcoming his last (present-day) nature by subjecting himself to himself and looking down upon — as from up above, to despise himself (from the Latin *dē□spicere* look down) — what is most and/or least despicable in his present kind.

Thus man has the nature of self-overcoming. Nietzsche calls the man who overcomes himself the "*Übermensch*." The *Übermensch* already exists, and Nietzsche's metaphysical thinking clearly saw it, but it is concealed from current views. Man as a rational animal is not yet completely rational; rather he is a passage, a transition, a bridge, a rope stretched over an abyss between the animal and the *Übermensch*. The *Übermensch* is the destination of the man who is 'passing over'. Zarathustra is only "the very first to pass over to him — he is the superman in the process of becoming." (Heidegger: 60). The *Übermensch* may be taken as a figure of translation and its meaning may be summed up in the following way:

1. The passage across;
2. The site from which the passage" takes leave;
3. "The site to which the passage goes."
    (Heidegger: 60)

All thought of the *Übermensch* must move in the multiplicity of its meanings. To understand what man, the last man, is as he has been till now, man needs to pass over, to separate himself from the last man he is. The *Übermensch* is quiet and does not appear in public places; he exists concealed because it is the stillest words that bring on the storm, and thoughts that come on doves' footsteps guide the world. The *Übermensch* thus passes over the last man.

Nietzsche thus negates existing morals and norms. His *Übermensch* is an ontogeny, the growth of the being of a human being. The *Übermensch* is a metabiological individual who includes principles of evaluation. It is the word and *logos,* a norm of development. Thus Nietzsche paints an icon of the individual composed of values. Values are what is valid. When that which is valid becomes no longer valid, like God, it ceases to exist. There is a need to rethink all values to resuscitate the divinity of man. Man himself is the one who is confronted with this challenge and who is destined to take it up. Such revaluation on man's part leads him to the *Übermensch*, to going *über*, 'above and beyond' himself.

## 3. Translators' Backgrounds

To have a better general understanding of the three translations of *Also sprach Zarathustra,* it is worthwhile to look behind the translations and examine the translators' backgrounds that shaped their worldviews.

Very little is known about Thomas Common (1850–1919), probably the first English translator of Nietzsche, who translated several of his books, including Nietzsche's masterpiece *Thus Spake Zarathustra.* He was a well-versed translator, critic and scholar who lived in the vicinity of Corstorphine, Scotland. He published his version of *Thus Spake Zarathustra* in 1909 — exactly one hundred years ago. The Thomas Common translation is today well-regarded by many readers and is one of the most widely read English translations of *Also sprach Zarathustra.* Thomas Common was extremely fascinated with Nietzsche's works, and in 1901 he published a study called *Nietzsche as Critic, Philosopher, Poet and Prophet.* From 1903 to 1916 Thomas Common issued a quarterly journal called *Notes for Good Europeans,* which was later titled *The Good European Point of View,* to increase public interest in Nietzsche.

Thomas Common's translation of Nietzsche was influenced by the translation method, dominant in the nineteenth century, "of eliding the linguistic and cultural difference of the foreign text" that "was firmly entrenched as a canon in English-language translation, always linked to a valorization of transparent discourse. The canonicity of domesticating translation was…beyond question." (Venuti: 76) The values of bourgeois society — "liberal and humanist, individualistic and elitist... — constrained the translator's activity." (Venuti: 81) Moreover, Common used archaisms (e.g., old verb forms such as "speaketh" and "spake") to make his translation sound more poetical and as if reaching from the past, like the Bible, thus attempting to imitate Nietzsche's biblical, prophetic style, using, for example, "Thus spake..." instead of "Thus spoke..." for *Also sprach...* Thus Common made his translation conform to nineteenth-century usage, which gave Nietzsche's *Übermensch* a poetical meaning, which will be discussed in this essay.

About fifty years later Walter Kaufmann (1921–1980), a German-American philosopher, poet, and translator of Nietzsche's works, reinstated "the older term, "overman"... to bring out the close relation between Nietzsche's conceptions of the *overman* and *self-overcoming,* and to recapture something of his rhapsodical play on the words "over" and "under," (as in 'go under' *untergehn*) particularly marked throughout the prologue," (Kaufmann: 115) considering such compound words as *Übermensch, überwunden, überreiches, überfliessen, überdruessig* that contain the significant German prefix *über-* to be most central to Nietzsche's *Also sprach Zarathustra.* Walter Kaufmann wrote a great deal on the issues of authenticity and death, on moral philosophy and existentialism, on theism and atheism, on Christianity and Judaism, as well as on the philosophy of literature. He was born in Freiburg, Germany in 1921, emigrated to America in 1939 and attended Williams College, where he majored in philosophy. Kaufmann was a renowned scholar and a translator of Nietzsche's works. His lucid English made

Nietzsche's works accessible to an English-speaking readership. He saw Nietzsche misunderstood as a great existentialist, and supported his scathing criticisms of Christianity. However, Kaufmann himself criticised Nietzsche's *Also sprach Zarathustra* for verbosity in some part of it, while admitting that it is "a mine of ideas... a major work of literature and a personal triumph" (Kaufmann: 111) and merits the title of a literary masterpiece.

Kaufmann, being a philosopher, offers a more accurately *philosophical* translation of Nietzsche (e.g., instead of Common's term "the baddest" for Nietzsche's *Böse* he uses "evil"), yet he replaces the archaic (and biblical) "speaketh," "spake," "thou," "thine," etc. found in Common's translation with the modern "speak(s)," "spoke," "you," and "your." He realizes that it is not necessary to choose "Thus *spake*" but simply "Thus *spoke*," because the biblical illusion is contained in the assertiveness of the whole combination *Also sprach* rather than in the single word *sprach*. On the one hand, Kaufmann domesticates, that is, contemporises (i.e., brings his translation closer to the modern times) his translation of *Also sprach*, for example; on the other, he foreignizes the term *Übermensch*, ("superman" in Common's translation) into "overman," which will be discussed in this essay. Thus, interestingly, by both domesticating and foreignizing his translation (where he feels necessary), Kaufmann brings a new, fluent, current (modern) translation of Nietzsche, which seems more "'natural,' i.e., not translated."(Venuti: 5) As to the term *superman*, the fact that it was rendered an inadmissible choice by the

1960s will be accounted for in the practical analysis of the translation.

Graham Parkes' translation of Nietzsche's *Also sprach Zarathustra* in 2005 superseded the Kaufmann translation. Graham Parkes, a contemporary philosopher and the only translator still living of the three, has taken a musical approach to translation of this work. His article entitled "The Symphonic Structure of *Thus Spoke Zarathustra*" talks at length about the musicality of Nietzsche's work. Nietzsche indeed wrote *Also sprach Zarathustra* under the influence of music. The reader feels carried away with the rolling waves of the symphonic ocean of *Also sprach Zarathustra* throughout the work and finds himself immersed in a deep, profound eternity of unfathomable existence. Parkes offers an "interpretive translation," which "should be seen as a transformation" (Venuti: 292), so bringing Nietzsche's work to itself in meaning. He renders *Also sprach Zarathustra* as a symphony consistent with Nietzsche's original. This also, in a way, affected the term *Übermensch*, while eliciting its exact meaning. Parkes, for example, preserves the German iambic cadence of *Ich lehre euch den Übermenschen* in his translation "I teach to you the *Overhuman*," while Common's and Kaufman's translations are not concerned with rendering the rhythmic flow: "I teach you the Superman" and "I teach you the *Overman*," respectively. Parkes, nevertheless, does not choose "I teach the Overhuman to you," which brings out the "you." Rather, he restructures the sentence so that the "Overhuman" comes to the fore, as the essence of the "you," i.e., humans.

## 4. Translation as Interpretation

Taking Lawrence Venuti's discussions of translation history in *The Translator's Invisibility* as guidance in approaching translation as an interpretation "process by which the chain of signifiers that constitutes the source-language text is replaced by a chain of signifiers in the target language" (Venuti: 17), it is important to remember, in this respect, that a translator is called upon to strike a balance between domesticating (in the sense of bending the translation toward contemporary usage and/or making it conform to the cultural and linguistic norms of the native (target) language) and foreignising the translation (in the sense of borrowing foreign words, for example, or making the translation conform to the norms or conventions of the foreign language, the language of the original). With this idea in mind, a glimpse into the essence of translation will be taken in the discussion below.

Translation literally means taking something at one place, carrying it across and putting it in another. In a literary sense the 'one place' would become the source text, the 'something' carried across — the words, ideas, values found in the source text, and the 'another place' — the destination, the target text, in which the form and content of the source text finds rest. A linguistic and cultural clash between the source and the target text takes place during the translation process. Such a battle of words, ideas and values is resolved, in my view, only when the target is actually hit at its innermost core. Once hit, the target text loses its 'targetness' altogether and becomes an original, only in a new light. Rather, it is the original that is the target in the light of a foreign language and culture. Thus, the source text becomes the target text. Yet, at the bottom "'the original' is superior to the translation." (Venuti: 307)

In the painstaking process of translation, the translator is called upon to perform one of the most challenging tasks of perceiving as receiving, rendering or conveying by means of, and manifesting through the foreign language and culture, the original words, ideas and values. Once arrived at their destination, these become adjusted to and transformed into the foreign language and culture. Foreign-language readers naturally perceive the translation not as a translation but as the original. They give little or no thought to "the translator's shadowy existence" (Venuti: 8), who the translator was and whose language they are reading. In reality, however, the ideas are the author's but the language is the translator's. Yet, the reader thinks of the text as the author's, not as the translator's. Thus, the role of the translator is reduced to that of being a fine, almost invisible, borderline between the original and its translation. Moreover, the author wins the praise and attention, while the translator has to accept this fact and live with it. The translator follows the author as a shadow. Yet, without this shadow, the author would not be known in a foreign language and culture.

Literary translation, on the whole, is an inspired creativity, a redefined, reborn originality, and at times a con-geniality; it is a *re-creation* of the genuine, unique original in a newly born original vernacular in its finitude. The infiniteness of the source text is manifested in multifaceted individual interpretations and translations.

The source text is one. The translations thereof are many. Which translation is truer to the original? This question requires further meditation.
Only that translation which is true, or faithful to the original is worthy of being called a translation. Here arise the following questions. What is 'true' in itself? What is the degree of 'trueness?' In what way can a translation be 'true' to the original? Would it be true to the original in meaning, rhythm, rhyme or some other mode of existence? These are the questions that do not readily receive an answer. Yet, the starting point in the direction of translation will be the original source text, the *source* of translation. All translation issues from its own source. This source can be nothing else but the original text in question. Indeed, the original text *is* in question — in fact, in many questions, at least in those ones posed above.
What is 'true' in itself and how is it related, if at all, to the source text? What is true about the source text is its essence, its essential, important, main core that is to be grasped in its entirety as it is and not as it is not. The trueness of the source text is determined by its existence outside itself, its effect or influence upon the surroundings. The first outsider will be the reader, the second, probably the translator, the third, the reader again but, strange as it may be, from 'a fourth world,' so to speak.
The first world in which the source text exists is the author's; the second, the native reader's; the third, the translator's; and, finally, the fourth, the native reader's again, or is it? Would the last native reader be a reader of the source text or of the translation thereof? This is the hardest question of all. Thus, as is seen, the source text

began by asking questions about itself in relation to truth and the degree of being true, ending up in its own translation. Is it justifiable, in this respect, to submit that there is a truth bridging the source text and its translation? What a link! But through what channels? The latter should be found in the source text again, for from it, and from it alone, does all energy flow.

Meaning (conceptuality), imagery (poeticism as expression of meaning), and sound (musicality as tone of meaning) lead one to think that meaning is the decisive component of all elements of the source text and of itself. Meaning is present throughout the whole essence of the original text. Meaning is omnipresent in the body of the original text. Meaning is that *core* of the original, the source of all sources. It is the centre-point of the text. Because it stands in the mean, it is *meaning*, for truth is at the middle as well. And, therefore, they are one. They are one at home with language, within language. Language, however, is the house of their being, of true meaning.

Language is that which secludes, and thus encompasses, the true golden meaning hidden in the source text. The task is to unearth this goldmine of loquacity. Words, phrases, images, rhythm and rhyme and other items of treasure would be a rare, sought-after find both for the reader and the translator, as well as for the reader of the translation. The translator's decisions reflect what he or she feels is worth bringing across.

Only by rendering meaning and every other manifestation of it in the language that clothes it in words can true meaning survive the journey from its source to another world. The source text is one. The translations are many. Which translation is truer to the original? The one that has a true meaning (which is a matter of subjective valuation and of being valid). True meaning allows for "generating an equivalent effect." (Venuti: 22)

True meaning is present in every unit of translation which is to be translated from the source language to the target language, and which inherently deals with equivalence and adequacy in the theory of literary translation. Equivalence presupposes correspondence of the unit of translation on the level of the phoneme, the morpheme, the word, a combination of words, the sentence, a combination of sentences, and the text. "The unit of translation is the *minimal* language unit in the source text that corresponds to an equivalent in the target text." (Barkhudarov: 40) Adequacy is concerned with conveying the basic communicative ideas, the nucleus component of them and a higher number of peripheral meanings thereof. Adequacy allows for more fluency in the translation. "The more fluent the translation, the more invisible the translator, and, presumably, the writer or meaning of the foreign text." (Venuti: 2)

Just as the *Übermensch* as a synthesis of art, philosophy and science (knowledge) is a man who is the author, re-evaluator and interpreter of his own ideas in art, philosophy, and science, so is the author of, the evaluating reader of, and the actual translator of the original in both literary (artistic) and philosophical (metaphysical; thinking), as well as scientific (linguistic) translation. The practical analysis of the translations of *Übermensch* will be carried out in the light of the above.

## 4. *Übermensch* as Superman, Overman and Overhuman

The term *Übermensch* is believed to have come into Nietzsche's works from Goethe. Sineokaya refers to Nietzsche as Goethe's spiritual, long-suffering son, upon whose heart weighs the sorrows of the whole century. Heidegger also believes that the term *Übermensch* was borrowed by Nietzsche from Goethe's *Faust*. According to Znamensky, Nietzsche gave this term the independent meaning elucidated above. (Znamensky: 78)

The problem of choosing between the terms Superman and Overman for the German *Übermensch* in English literature is still current. Each translator views it differently and chooses the most suitable variant, in his opinion, to convey the meaning adequately.

The prefix "über-", in Nietzsche's context, means 'beyond, over and above,' while presupposing elevation, exaltation and improvement of the human species. The *Übermensch* is something that goes beyond the notion of humankind as that which is overcome.

No part of *Also sprach Zarathustra* can be detached from the whole body of the work, for, if separated, Zarathustra's teachings will disintegrate into incompleteness. There is a fine thread of thought running through the fabric of this masterpiece, in the very manner or style of expressing original ideas. This style is that of a poet. And poetry is only considered magnificent and polished only when no part, no phrase, nor even a word can ever be removed from it, for to remove it would strip the content bare of the fine clothing that poetry is. There is

35

so much poetry inherent in Nietzsche's work that this poetry itself becomes the philosophy it expresses: "you exuberant star!" (Common: 3); "you overrich star!" (Kaufmann: 122) How about the original German? – *du überreiches Gestirn!* (Nietzsche) Does this majestic *überreiches*, "overrich" and especially "exuberant" not sound both poetical and philosophical (or even imperial[10])? What meaning — philosophical or poetical — is primary here? Or is it a combination of the two, since "over" directly suggests the overcoming of man in order become Overman? If this word poses itself to the reader's understanding as simply an adjective having no particular meaning or just a word to fill in the gap between *du* and *Gestirn*, or between the corresponding "you" and "star" in the translations, then the following counter question on the reader's part may also arise: Why should there be a gap at all? How should, in this case, such a gap or lack thereof be confronted on its merits? Obviously, the star (*Gestirn*), which is the poetic word for "sun" (*die Sonne*), can exist in Zarathustra's thinking only as something hot, golden, abundant, exuberant, overflowing and overrich. Already in the very first lines in the prologue the German prefix *über-*, the English equivalent "over-," is recurrent in such words as *überdrüssig* ("overtired," though not found in Walter Kaufman's or Thomas Common's translation; whereas Graham Parkes translates it as "overburdened" (Parkes: 9), and thereby preserves the recurrent "over-"), *überfliessen* ("overflow" (Common: 3-4; Kaufmann: 122; Parkes: 9)

---

[10] *Reich* (in *überreiches*) as rich and empire may also suggest affluent, imperial power.

present in all three translations) and later, as the prologue progresses, in such words as *Übermenschen*, ("Superman," (Common: 6) "Overman" (Kaufmann: 124) and finally Overhuman (Parkes: 11)) and *überwunden* ("surpass," (Common: 6); "overcome" (Kaufman: 124; Parkes: 11)). How poetic, how prophetic this recurrence is! How transcendental, how conceptual its grip *is* over a human being's essence! So much will to power is exercised by this *über-*, or "over-," over the human soul. It compels and impels, lures and allures man to self-surpassing and self-overcoming.

Common adequately renders *überreiches* as "exuberant," which sounds very deep and much more poetical and may be said to be semantically transformed, for it captures not only the meaning of being profuse and abundant but also that of being enthusiastic, happy and blessed as it pertains to the Star to be, especially in Nietzsche's context. Also, it consists of four syllables and is very close acoustically to the German *überreiches*. Three out of four syllables have a syllabic resemblance: "-u-be-re(i)-," and at least five out of eight sounds have a phonemic resemblance: "-u-b-e-r-e-." Because of Common's splendid rendering of the syllabic and phonemic flow in English, the rhythm is also closely preserved in the translation, which elicits and conveys the symphony inherent in the structure of this word combination. Thus, the Thomas Common translation of *überreiches* as "exuberant" accentuates the poetic meaning of this term. Common, imbued with a heightened feeling of enthusiasm, makes a departure from the literal translation of *überreiches* as "overrich" toward a more personalized perception of it as being plentifully joyful, rather than blissfully abundant. The deep joy and bliss, the excessive happiness of the smiling sun, as Common individually perceives it, led him to choose "exuberant." This example clearly shows that Common did not prefer the literal translation and probably underestimated the significance of Nietzsche's allusion to the *über*, present in the *Übermensch* and recurrent in other words, such as *überwunden* and *überfliessen*, and took it as an independent word, having no correlative significance in Nietzsche's context. Yet, by rendering *überreiches* poetically, he fortunately brought out its poetical connotations that Nietzsche meant to be hidden in the *Übermensch*, who is understood as an artist in one of his creative manifestations.

The Walter Kaufman translation of *überreiches* as "overrich" is undeniably literal and hence preserves and strongly elicits the philosophical meaning of *Übermensch*, for it uses the prefix "over-", just as Nietzsche does *über* in *überreiches*, thereby alluding to the meaning of going beyond, over and above humankind, implicit in the original *Übermensch*, as well as in his own translation of it as *Overman*. Kaufmann thus makes a shift toward Nietzsche's metaphysical philosophy by his translation of *überreiches* as "overrich," as compared to Common, who views Nietzsche primarily as an artist. Kaufmann's "overrich" is the closest variant of *überreiches* that a translator can come up with, so providing not only an adequate but also an equivalent translation of it on the level of the word and the morpheme. Yet its adequacy primarily depends on its equivalency which consists in the compoundedness of the word: "over-" and "-rich," just as *über-* and *-reiches*. Most importantly, Kaufman's "over" is repeatedly preserved to allude to his term "Overman." For *Übermensch* and "Superman" and "Overman" are as "exuberant" and "overrich" in wisdom and blessedness as is the *überreiches* Star in light.

Graham Parkes, being a philosopher, like Walter Kaufmann, follows him in his steps and uses "overrich," thus re-affirming the human transcendence implied in the German *überreiches*, in the overrichness of the star, indicative of the human potential sufficient to breach boundaries and limitations of traditional understanding of self-essence in the way of transforming the kind of humankind that it is into an over-kind of the kind, into what it is destined to become.

As to the term *Übermensch*, Common's translation of it as "Superman" does not capture the full meaning of a self-overcoming man, as a man who is over, above and beyond himself. It is relevant to mention here Bernard Shaw's play *Man and Superman*, written in 1903. Shaw uses "Superman" as a translation of Nietzsche's *Übermensch* to show that "man is the spiritual creator, whereas woman is the biological "life force" that must always triumph over him." This play must have influenced Common's translation of *Also sprach Zarathustra*, since he was familiar with this work before he published his translation in 1909, six years after Shaw's play had been published. Whether it is Shaw's or Common's translation of the term *Übermensch*, it is Common who used it in his translation of Nietzsche's work. It is suggested that this term be further considered as Common's translation. The prefix *super-* implies excessiveness, excellence and, at most, superiority (literally in the sense of 'aboveness,' as the opposite of *sub-*) and 'superman' therefore sounds rather poetic than philosophical in Common's translation. It also has some funny associations with the muscled comic character Superman from the cartoon series (originally conceived as a villain after the pattern of the Nazi-compromised *Übermensch* ("Superman"), but later transformed into a saviour of the world, after Nietzsche's philosophy began to be appreciated on its mertis). Evidently Common was not influenced by a character not yet in existence, in the American film *Superman*, in which Christopher Reeve plays the part of the fantastical extraterrestrial superhero who saves humanity from exraterrestrial evil. This term *superman* in fact was coined in 1900–09 as the translation of the German *Übermensch*, prior to the film. And Common was probably the first to have translated it as *Superman*. However, the poetical content that it contains supersedes any of those contained in Kaufmann's version, "Overman", or Parkes' translation, "Overhuman."

Parkes' version "Overhuman" exceeds the German original *Übermensch* by one syllable and in a way sounds compounded, overengineered and complex, whereas *Übermensch*, while not taken lightly at all, is supposed to proceed as easily and prophetically, as from the mouth of God, which is also true of the tri-syllabic "Superman" and "Overman." "Superman" comes closest to the *Übermensch* acoustically, containing five out of six original sounds "-u-b/p-e-m-e," with one sound variance; whereas "Overman" is the closest variant from the philosophical point of view, namely presupposing overcoming of man, yet slightly hinting with its composition at the acoustic resemblance as well: five out of six sounds are transmitted sufficiently entirely from the source language to the target language: "-o/u-v/b-e-m-e-," with the two first undergoing phonetic variations.

On the whole all the three translators have translated *Übermensch* adequately. Yet Thomas Common, unlike Walter Kaufmann and Graham Parkes, renders *überwunden* as *surpass*, giving preference to the French synonym *surpasser*, thus losing the linking allusion to the Germanic *über-*. *Surpassing*, while an adequate translation of *überwunden* is not equivalent on the level of the morpheme. Yet it has other value in itself is that, since it is originally a French borrowing, it is presupposed to have implicitly a more elevated — and hence more poetic — meaning found in high style of language.

However, neither Common nor Kaufmann rid their "-man" of the masculine connotation inherent in both *Superman* and *Overman* respectively. Only Parkes succeeds in doing so by using *Overhuman* for *Übermensch*. The absence of any gender connotation in the rendering of the German gender-neutral *Übermensch* is significant for the English version of Nietzsche's *Also sprach Zarathustra*, for this work is intended for all humanity, both men and women, as well as for none at the same time: the subtitle *Ein Buch für Alle und Keinen* makes it clear. Nietzsche means by his subtitle that one may become worthy of reading this book only by transcending one's self with this book. By no means does Nietzsche use *Übermensch* to refer to either men or men in particular, for the very morpheme "-mensch" connotes the meaning of the English equivalent 'human,' which, once heard, has ready associations with *humankind, humanity* and *human beings*, rather than *male, gentleman, manly* and *masculine.*

Would Nietzsche himself have used *Overman* or *Overhuman* had he written in English at the end of the nineteenth century? Of course, he, being a philosopher, would have preferred "over" to "super" to make allusions to such common English words — and central to his work — as "overcome," "overflow," and "overtired" or "overburdened,"[11] also if he were to write *Also sprach Zarathustra* today. "Over" is rather the opposite of "under" (*unter*) in the meaning of going *under* (*untergehn* and *Untergang*), going *down*, declining, collapsing, which is suggestive of decadent nihilism, "the last man," and bad instincts than "sub" (which is of Latin origin, meaning 'below,' 'beneath' (something that is above) which is the opposite of "super" (as in superior, supervision, superintendent). Moreover, such words as superior (as a master, which is antonymous with "inferior" (as a slave)), supervision and superintendent would have definitely suggested command and (Christian) master and slave morality to Nietzsche, of which he was a sworn enemy (as is evidenced, for example, in his *Antichrist*) and would not therefore have appealed to him as allusions (possibly made

---

[11] Editor's note: It is interesting to note that all these terms *can* also be expressed by compounds containing 'super-' — e.g., 'supersede' (cf. also 'suppress', 'surmount'), 'superfluity' (at least in the sense of 'overflow' as a noun), 'super-tired' and 'super-burdened' (at least in today's vernacular).

by the term *superman* that nevertheless has the poetical meaning in Common's translation). Above all, the philosophical connotations of "over," if put on a scale, would have outweighed the poetical (to say nothing of possible moralistic) ones of "super." As regards the German "-mensch," — since "humankind," "humanity," "the human race" all have no gender implications and do not therefore confuse the English mind that it is the nature of a *human* being, not the nature of a *male* or a *female*, that is in relationship with the Being of beings, — Nietzsche would have preferred "-human," but only, possibly, if he were to write today, for the term *man*[12] has met with objection in recent years on the grounds of its sex-marked denotatum. The nineteenth century would not have prevented Nietzsche from using "-man," for it was quite common historically for "-man" to refer to both men and women, for example in compound words that designate specific occupations (*foreman*; *mailman*; *policeman*; *repairman*; etc.), that were later dropped in favour of gender-neutral terms in the *Dictionary of Occupational Titles* published by the U.S. Department of Labor in 1977. The dictionary terms for the occupations mentioned above are *supervisor, mail* or *letter carrier, police officer* (or just *officer*), *repairer* (as in *radio repairer*). (Random Dictionary)

Other options for the German *Übermensch* may be suggested for consideration: *Superhuman, Aboveman,*

---

[12] See John Woodsworth's discussion of the term *man* in his Translator's Preface to Book 1 of the Ringing Cedars Series: http://www.ringingcedars.com/materials/book-1-preface.pdf

*Abovehuman, Beyondman, Beyondhuman.* The flexibility of the linguistic norms of the English language allows, as is seen, for more translation variants of the *Übermensch*. But none of the latter may seem to be ultimately acceptable poetically. However, *Abovehuman* and *Beyondhuman* could both serve as options but only in the sense of 'higher than' or 'outside of,' or 'to the farther side of, or 'more distant than' a human being, respectively, whereas "over" captures both 'above and beyond' in *Overhuman* or *Overman*. Finally, transliteration and/or transcription could serve as an option to eliminate the problem of translating the *Übermensch* by simply rendering it in English as *Übermensch*. To choose this option, however, could be considered a failure on the translator's part and/or a 'foreignization' of the English language.

Thus, the three different translation variants *Superman*, *Overman*, and *Overhuman* only reinterpret the *Übermensch* as a synthesis of art (poetry, images), philosophy (thinking will to power) and knowledge or science (language). Despite this important difficulty in the translation of *Also sprach Zarathustra*, Nietzsche's work still remains the greatest gift that has ever been given to human beings. As Nietzsche himself writes of *Also sprach Zarathustra*:

> With [*Also sprach Zarathustra*] I have given mankind the greatest present that has ever been made to it so far. This book, with a voice bridging centuries, is not only the highest book there is, the book that is truly characterized by the air of the heights — the whole fact of man lies *beneath* it at a tremendous distance — it is

also the *deepest*, born out of the innermost wealth of truth, an inexhaustible well to which no pail descends without coming up again filled with gold and goodness. (*Ecce Homo*, *Preface*, §4)[13]

## Conclusion

The three different translations of the term *Übermensch* as *Superman*, *Overman* and *Overhuman* bring to the fore the three constituents of the concept of *Übermensch*: artist, philosopher and scientist (philologist). The Thomas Common translation is a more poetic, classical interpretation of the *Übermensch* as a creative, artistic human being. The Walter Kaufmann translation is more philosophically accurate, in the context of Nietzsche's philosophy with a historical sense (of the human being as ontogeny) than the Thomas Common version, whereas the Graham Parkes translation is more equivalently rendered linguistically and contemporarily strips *Übermensch* bare of gender connotations to refer to all humanity, to the will to power as the creative essence of a human being in general and in particular, irrespective of gender, thereby re-affirming the *Übermensch* as a scientist, a scholar, and a philologist.

Thus, all three translation variants — *Superman*, *Overman* and *Overhuman* — complement Nietzsche's artistic, thinking and knowledgeable *Übermensch*, the highest manifestation of the all-encompassing will to power and eternal return of the same.

---

[13] Kaufmann's translation.

## Works Cited

Barkhudarov, Leonid "The Problem of the Unit of Translation," ed. Susan Bassnett and André Lefevere *Translation as Social Action: Russian and Bulgarian Perspectives*, ed. and tr. Palma Zlateva, London and New York: Routledge, 1993, p. 40.

Bely, Andrei "Friedrich Nietzsche" *Smysl iskusstva. Simvolism kak miroponimanie ("seria Mysliteli XX veka") [The Meaning of Art. Symbolism as Interpretation of the World* series *The $20^{th}$ Century Thinkers]*, Moscow: Politizdat, 1994, p. 182, www.lib.ru .

Heidegger, Martin *Nietzsche* ed. & tr. David Farrell Krell, HarperSanFrancisco *A division of* Harper Collins *Publishers*: 1991, Vol. 4, p. 6.

___. *What is Called Thinking?* tr. J. Glenn Gray, Perennial, An Imprint of HarperCollins *Publishers*: 2004, p. 58, 60.

Nietzsche, Friedrich *The Portable Nietzsche* tr. Walter Kaufmann, New York: The Viking Press, 1954, pp. 111, 115, 122, 124; Ecce Homo, *Preface, §4*;

___. *Also Sprach Zarathustra* The Project Gutenberg EBook, release date: January, 2005 [EBook #7205] http://www.gutenberg2000.de/nietzsche/zara/also.htm;

___. *Thus Spake Zarathustra* tr. Thomas Common, *The Complete Works of Friedrich Nietzsche*, ed. Dr. Oscar Levy, New York: Russell & Russell•Inc, 1964, V.11, pp. 3-4, 6;

___. *Thus Spoke Zarathustra* tr. Graham Parkes, Oxford: Oxford World's, 2005, p.9,11. *Random House Webster's Unabridged Dictionary* software, Lernout & Hauspie™: 1999, entry "man."

Shaw, Bernard *Man and Superman* Cambridge, Mass.: The University Press: 1903, New York: 1999. http://www.bartleby.com/157/.

Sineokaya, Y.V. "Rubezh vekov: russkaya sud'ba Sverkhcheloveka Nietzsche" ["The Intersection of the Centuries: The Russian Fate of Nietzsche's Overman"] *Fridrikh Nitsshe i filosofia v Rossii (sbornik statey)* [*Friedrich Nietzsche and Russian Philosophy* (a collection of articles)], Saint Petersburg: Izdatel'stvo Russkogo Khristianskogo gumanitarnogo instituta, 1999, e-text.

Venuti, Lawrence *The Translator's Invisibility* ed. Susan Bassnett, André Lefevere, London and New York: Routledge, 1995, pp. 2, 5, 8, 17, 22, 76, 81, 187, 188, 292, 307.

Znamensky, S. "'Sverkhchelovek' Nitssche" *Vera i Razum* ["Nietzsche's Overman," *Faith and Reason*], 1909, #3/4, p. 78.

# Nietzsche: Translation as Perspectivism
(2010)

## Introduction

In *Western Translation Theory: From Herodotus to Nietzsche*, Douglas Robinson writes:

> "Nietzsche's passing remarks on translation from *The Gay Science* and *Beyond Good and Evil* are not particularly original, but hold interest as late-nineteenth-century examples of romanticism that point ahead to the hermeneutical translation-theories of twentieth-century thinkers like Benjamin and Buber, Heidegger and Gadamer, Steiner and Derrida." (262)

In my judgement, to appreciate Nietzsche's remarks on translation in those two works of his, one has to really think through Nietzsche's conception of translation within the context of his philosophy. The goal of this paper is to unfold Nietzsche's conception of *Übersetzung* within the larger context of his notion of truth. It is argued that by translating the human being back to his or her original nature, Germans are able to translate the life-invigorating tempo of the style of the original text and thereby liberate themselves from Schopenhauerian pessimism, becoming what they are, i.e., German, or good Europeans.

Nietzsche's critique of philosophy or knowledge in general on the basis of metaphorical language, bodily participation and truth as an aesthetic element of perspectivism is inseparable from his critique of translation, because both philosophy and translation seek to interpret reality. Moreover, the translation is a double form of interpretation, because it also interprets the original, which is already an interpretation of reality. Since Nietzsche scathingly critiques truth in philosophy and views it as a falsification of reality, translation cannot bypass the same critique of his and must therefore be viewed as a falsification of the original text as well. Yet Nietzsche, it will be shown, by introducing (in place of truth) *art* as the only truthful element of perspectival interpretations of reality, thereby makes the unity of the German nation a possibility.

## 2. The Truth of Reality and Translation

A one-sided, divine, 'truthful' interpretation of existence is conducive to a falsification of human nature. Truthful interpretation should be questioned. In the opening line of *Jenseits von Gute und Böse* (JGB) (1886), Nietzsche compares truth with a woman: „Vorausgesetzt, daß die Wahrheit ein Weib ist —, wie?" (JGB Vorrede) What he means by his supposition is that truth is fickle and changeable, weak and seductive, just like a woman. It does not let it itself be won by men. Dogmatic philosophers who have been chasing truth as men do women, have failed to grasp it. By *truth* Nietzsche, of course, means, first and foremost, the Christian truth. Nietzsche posits truth as *woman* between reality and philosopher-men who are trying to understand reality.

Nietzsche's search for truth and his perspectivism and criticisms of the pursuit of truth as an ascetic ideal (in *Zur*

*Genealogie der Moral* (1887)) must depend on the possibility of the existence of some truth. He develops his conception of will to power and eternal return in *Also sprach Zarathustra* (1883 – 1886) and *Jenseits von Gute und Böse* which seem to reject metaphysics, because they lay the foundation for an alternative ideal to the ascetic ideal, on which the whole of metaphysics has rested throughout the entire history of European philosophy. Now, to contend that Nietzsche did deny the existence of truth (like Danto or Derrida) threatens the basis on which Nietzsche critiqued Christian (ascetic) morality, for example. That is, the critique or denial of the existence of truth takes place only *on the basis of some truth,* which for Nietzsche is the truth of perspectivism. It follows that if human nature is viewed only as divine or 'truthful', i.e., as stable and fixed, as in the traditional Christian sense, then the bodily, animal nature of the human being is not taken into consideration. The denial of bodily participation as valuable for divine creativity results in a falsification of the original text of human nature as animal nature. The healthy animal nature of the human being is the condition for healthy divine, creative life. The values of divine existence should, therefore, not be at variance with the animal instincts and forces of the human being. Human drives are the inexhaustible source of life energy unfolding in multiple individual, unique, perspectival, divine interpretations of existence.

Since the original text is one kind of interpretation of existence, reality may suffer a falsification if the original is not further interpreted by translation but remains forever 'true'. The truth of translation should be questioned paralleling the truth of existence as discussed above. Inasmuch as philosophy or knowledge is a reflection of reality, translation is a reflection of the original. In translation, truth as woman is first posited between reality and the original before it is posited between the original and its translation. The connection or relation between them all is weak, respectively. There is so much 'Christianity' between the original and the reality it describes, and even more weakness between the original and its translation that to claim the truth or correctness of the translation is an absurdity.

Language may have been one of the misleading obstacles in chasing truth. According to Christian J. Emden's discussion of Nietzsche's view of language as metaphor in his *Nietzsche on Language, Consciousness, and the Body*,[14] Maudemarie Clark's claim[15] that the mature Nietzsche believed that knowledge of truth can be obtained and that he accepted the correspondence theory of truth, may utterly fail if one takes into consideration Nietzsche's account of *metaphor*. For Nietzsche, metaphor is a rhetorical phenomenon intrinsic to all linguistic and, therefore, scientific representations. If all language is metaphor, however, then the concept of metaphor itself collapses, as it can no longer mark a distinction in linguistic categories. However, Nietzsche embraces both

---

[14] Christian J. Emden. *Nietzsche on Language, Consciousness, and the Body*. Urbana: University of Illinois Press, 2005.
[15] Maudemarie Clark. *Nietzsche on Truth and Philosophy*. Modern European Philosophy. New York: Cambridge University Press, 1990.

the philosophical significance of a rhetorical problem and the rhetorical element as inherent in language (as opposed to Plato and Locke, who consider eloquence as inappropriate to philosophy). But, since for Nietzsche rhetorical elements do not bear a strict correspondence to reality — because language for him is as an organic process — there arises the question of how communication (and, in our case, translation) is possible. Nietzsche's response is that metaphor is a means of transferring signs between humans. Signs, however, do not directly correspond to reality. Therefore, communication is forever *indeterminate*. This indeterminacy is emphasised by physiological processes. Metaphor and physiology meet in memory, the seat of human consciousness. It follows that the human mind is a product of human physiology inseparable from the need for communication. Nietzsche's metaphorical account of memory, language, and consciousness, thanks to which knowledge, mind, and society are possible, should be understood as a legitimate effort to synthesise the complex terms of the persistent mind-body problem. Since communication and translation are necessarily connected, the indeterminacy of communication renders the translation of the original, which is in itself already a kind of indeterminate communication, even more indeterminate than the original text.

Furthermore, the indeterminacy of translation denies the translation itself the possibility of being an effect of the original. All relations are consequences of the essences of things, not their essences. (Schrift 381) A metaphor comes into existence when cause and effect become identified.

Analogically, if translation is a kind of metaphor of the original, the translation is a consequence of the essence of the original, not the original itself. Since, also, the original is the consequence of the essence of the reality which it seeks to describe, the translation is double the consequence, i.e., it is also the consequence of the essence of the reality which the original describes. Effects are not causes, as much as translations are not originals. Since both the translation of the original and the original itself strive to describe one and the same reality, while the translation at the same time seeks to reinterpret the original — and thus both are inexact (the translation is even more inexact) — the distinction made between the original and its translation — that the original cannot be called the cause of the translation, nor can the translation be termed the effect of the original — should remain conscious of the similarity between them in this, that they both falsify the reality they describe. This needs to be pursued further.

In light of the above, I think that Nietzsche would go so far as to say that translation is not only an inexact representation of the original but also a falsification thereof. "It is this falsified world of 'conceptual mummies' that occupies the philosophers: 'Philosophy, as I alone still admit, as the universal form of history, as the attempt to somehow describe and abbreviate in signs Heraclitean becoming (as if *translated* and mummified in a type of apparent Being [*Sein*])' (Nietzsche *KGW* VII, 3: 36127)." (Schrift 386) Therefore, whenever a human being creates, he or she creates a falsified world. It follows that the original is a falsification of reality and the translation of the original is a falsification of the 'original' falsification

53

of reality, therefore (necessarily) of the original as well. Thus the translation is a double falsification of reality.

Furthermore, Nietzsche writes: " 'Language, it seems, was invented only for what is average, medium, communicable. With language, the speaker immediately vulgarizes himself' (*GD* "Skirmishes of an Untimely Man" 26)." (Schrift 389) It follows that, since translation is also one kind of interpretation of the original, thereby of existence, the original text suffers a falsification if it is viewed as the 'original', 'truthful', divine text, i.e., as stable and fixed. In this regard the truth of the 'truth' of translation should be questioned.

Any critique of truth is a perspective interpretation that already presupposes an established belief, which largely depends on our *affects* or *drives*, according to Nietzsche (*On the Genealogy of Morals* III, 12). These affects or drives are embodied and influence human understanding of reality. Bodily participation in representations of things extends to all activities of the mind. Translation is one of them. In fact, representation of things involves translation of those things together with human affects or drives into the realm of perspectivism. Translational perspectivism is in itself an interpretation of things and cognitive activities. Analogically, human affects or drives are admixed to the translation of the original text, which is already an affected representation of reality. From this it follows that translation of the original text is subject to perspectivism. The beauty of it all is that perspectivism is inseparable from translation, for there is an aesthetic element in the activity of translation which, I believe, is posited by Nietzsche as truth.

Nietzsche would agree that translation claims that it has access to truth in striving to communicate the original to the foreign reader, for it strives to grasp the whole and fix it as truth. Truths are necessary to make life and knowledge possible, but since they are uncertain or false, they should not be relied upon. The aesthetic criterion, however, is more important than truth, for it is the creative drive. This choice of aesthetic criteria is, for Nietzsche, one of necessity, for the criteria by which to judge correctness or certainty are not available to man: " 'the correct perception – which would mean the adequate expression of the object in a subject – as a contradictory impossibility: for between two absolutely different spheres, as between subject and object, there is no causality, no correctness, no expression: there is, at most an *aesthetic* relation' (Nietzsche *MA* VI: 85; *KGW* III, 9: 379; *WL* 1, 86)." (Schrift 378) In this context, the original text should be regarded as an aesthetic relation between the subject (the writer) and the object (the reality that the writer describes). The translation of such an original text is the aesthetic relation between the translator as agent or subject and the original as object. The truth of translation as an aesthetic element can find itself at home in the very multiplicity of translations of the original text, i.e., in their perspectivism. Moreover, the more perspectives we have, the better we are as persons, as individuals. Likewise, Nietzsche would say that the more perspectival translations or translational perspectives we have, the better we are as practical translators or translation theorists.

What follows from the above discussion is that the denial of the translator's bodily participation, as valuable for divine creativity, results in a falsification of both the original text and the original text of human existence as divine, true, stable and fixed (whereas they both are, in fact, affected by the animal characteristics of the human being). The healthy animal nature of the writer of the original text is the first condition for a healthy, divine translation of the original. The second condition for a healthy, divine translation of the healthy original text is the healthy animal nature of the translator. Therefore, the values of a divine translation of the original should not be in contradiction with the animal instincts and forces of both the translator and the writer of the original text. Finally, the human drives of the translator are an inexhaustible source of creative energy unfolding in multiple individual, unique, perspectival, divine interpretations of the original text, which should be subject to the same healthy qualities of the writer of the original.

From the above discussion of the nature of translation in the context of Nietzsche's critique of truth it follows that a healthy interpretation of existence is conducive to a healthy translation of the original. At the core of the healthy interpretation of existence is a realisation of being as becoming, which leads to multiple perspectival interpretations of existence, whereas at the core of a healthy translation lies the *running*, life-invigorating tempo of the style of the original, according to Nietzsche. The larger notion of Nietzsche's *Übersetzung* is the translation of the human being from a one-sided 'divine', Christian interpretation of human nature back to its original text, its animal nature and re-creation of all values on the basis of truth as affirmation of life through *art*, thereby overcoming

Schopenhauerian pessimism overwhelming the whole of Europe and emancipating the Germans lacking Germanity from the Christian narrow-mindedness, thus helping them become a united German nation, i.e., good Europeans, within the unity of Europe. In this regard, a healthy translation following the dechristianisation of the German race is a great tool in delivering the Germans from Schopehauerian pessimism by adopting the free-spirited style of translating from the Romans. This will be discussed in more detail below.

### 3. What is a Healthy Translation?

Truth is an ideal constructed by philosopher-men. It cannot *not* be created. It has to be created in order to somehow represent reality so that one can orient oneself in it. Human beings are ideal-makers, because they are bodies and have differences. As bodies, they create images of themselves — i.e., they translate themselves into images they thus become. Moreover, they act according to their 'translations'. The truth of the images humans translate themselves into must be re-evaluated within the context of body. Nietzsche's going beyond *Gute* and Böse in *Jenseits von Gute und Böse*, does not mean that those conceptions should be eliminated. On the contrary, they should be re-evaluated on the basis of bodily participation in the creation of values and held accountable to the bodies they are enabling humans to become. Thus, as Zarathustra says, human beings should "remain faithful to the earth" (*The Portable Nietzsche* (PN) 188–189). The earth as a body will give birth to the *Übermensch* if Zarathustra, who after descending the mountain in search of his children (PN 438), in Oppel's interpretation, enters into an interdependence with woman. From this it follows that since ideals live in bodies, humans are called upon to cultivate a physiological perspective that would see values as expressions of health. Healthy ideals would refine senses, strengthen human instincts and release creative energies.[16] Since ideals would involve all kinds of translations as human valuations of the original text, translations, then, must agree with bodily health. What does a healthy translation mean, after all? I think that for Nietzsche it would mean to be able to render the tempo of the original.

In the following passage on translation from *Jenseits von Gute und Böse*, Nietzsche expressly says that what is most difficult in translation to render is the *tempo* of the style of the original. Moreover, he believes that one fails to preserve the original tempo when translating into German. The reason for it, I believe Nietzsche thinks, is the serious, thoughtful mentality of the German race affected by Christian morality. With the loss of tempo, unique, individual *nuances* of the original are unfortunately never conveyed and the translation thus becomes merely a simplification, vulgarisation and falsification of the original text. He writes:

---

[16] LaMothe, Kimerer L. "Nietzsche on Gender: Beyond Man and Woman." *Hypatia* 22.3 (2007): 194 – 197. *Project Muse*. Web. 19 Nov. 2010.

Was sich am schlechtesten aus einer Sprache in die andere übersetzen läßt, ist das tempo ihres Stils: als welcher im Charakter der Rasse seinen Grund hat, physiologischer gesprochen, im Durchschnitts-tempo ihres „Stoffwechsels". Es gibt ehrlich gemeinte Übersetzungen, die beinahe Fälschungen sind, als unfreiwillige Vergemeinerungen des Originals, bloß weil sein tapferes und lustiges tempo nicht mit übersetzt werden konnte, welches über alles Gefährliche in Dingen und Worten wegspringt, weghilft. Der Deutsche ist beinahe des Presto in seiner Sprache unfähig: also, wie man billig schließen darf, auch vieler der ergötzlichsten und verwegensten Nuances des freien, freigeisterischen Gedankens. So gut ihm der Buffo und der Satyr fremd ist, in Leib und Gewissen, so gut ist ihm Aristophanes und Petronius unübersetzbar. Alles Gravitätische, Schwerflüssige, Feierlich-Plumpe, alle langwierigen und langweiligen Gattungen des Stils sind bei den Deutschen in überreicher Mannichfaltigkeit entwickelt... (JGB §28)

The term *Durchschnitts* Nietzsche uses for 'average' literally means 'cut through' and it directly refers to "*Stoffwechsels*" ('exchange of substance resulting in release of energy'), which suggests that the tempo of the style of the original is essentially inherent in the bodily constitution of the race. As is evident, the original, according to Nietzsche, cannot be thought of merely in intellectual, metaphysical concepts, but it finds its grounds in the very physiology of the writer (and the translator). Further, in order for a German to translate (to Nietzsche's standards) a text that would have the tempo of Aristophanes' or Petronius' works, he or she must have the same physiological constitution. Therefore, it is evident that Nietzsche grounds translation in physiology, that is, in body. Further, Nietzsche makes an exception for Lessing, whom he considers a free spirit, yet he immediately denies the German language and Lessing's prose the possibility of imitating the galloping tempo of Machiavelli's "Principe":

> Lessing macht eine Ausnahme ...... Lessing liebte auch im tempo die Freigeisterei, die Flucht aus Deutschland. Aber wie vermöchte die deutsche Sprache, und sei es selbst in der Prosa eines Lessing, das tempo Macchiavell's nachzuahmen, der, in seinem principe, die trockne feine Luft von Florenz athmen lässt und nicht umhin kann, die ernsteste Angelegenheit in einem unbändigen Allegrissimo vorzutragen: vielleicht nicht ohne ein boshaftes Artisten-Gefühl davon, welchen Gegensatz er wagt, — Gedanken, lang, schwer, hart, gefährlich, und ein tempo des Galopps und der allerbesten muthwilligsten Laune. (JGB §28)

Nietzsche likewise denies the German language the capacity to translate the works of Petronius: "Wer endlich dürfte gar eine deutsche Übersetzung des Petronius wagen, der ... ... die Füsse eines Windes hat, den Zug und Athem, den befreienden Hohn eines Windes, der Alles gesund macht, indem er Alles laufen macht!" (JGB §28). The remedy for the sickness of the German language will be found further on. For now, as is evident, the significance of health in any text is crucial to Nietzsche's understanding of translation in general.

As has been shown, Nietzsche makes the point that the German language, as well as the German-speaking people, because they are ones who speak it, lacks a joyful, ironic tempo in translation. Such a tempo, Nietzsche would say, is necessary for a light-spirited translation that would enhance human life and exalt the spirit of the individual. Even Plato, whom Nietzsche critiques among other wise philosophers, and who repudiated Greek life, could not do without a book of Aristophanes (JGB §28), for he desired to engage in lively irony, apart from his moral discussions of truth, good, beauty, virtue and justice. In order to harness the tempo, Nietzsche would propose *Selbstüberwindung*. This has to be looked at more closely.

### 4. Translation as Self-Conquest

As fully unchristian beings, the Romans viewed translation as (self-) conquest, according to Nietzsche. This is what he sees to be lacking in the Germans, as prone to Schopenauerian pessimism, as will be demonstrated below.

Nietzsche provides another short passage on translation in *Die Fröhliche Wissenschaft*. (FW) §83 (1882) To cite the larger part of the passage would help the reader to contrast the free-spiritedness of the Romans against the sluggishness of the Germans.

> Übersetzungen. — Man kann den Grad des historischen Sinnes, welchen eine Zeit besitzt, daran abschätzen, wie diese Zeit Übersetzungen macht und

vergangene Zeiten und Bücher sich einzuverleiben sucht.... Und das römische Alterthum selbst: wie gewaltsam und naiv zugleich legte es seine Hand auf alles Gute und Hohe des griechischen älteren Alterthums! Wie übersetzten sie in die römische Gegenwart hinein! Wie verwischten sie absichtlich und unbekümmert den Flügelstaub des Schmetterlings Augenblick! So übersetzte Horaz hier und da den Alcäus oder den Archilochus, so Properz den Callimachus und Philetas (Dichter gleichen Ranges mit Theokrit, wenn wir urtheilen dürfen): was lag ihnen daran, dass der eigentliche Schöpfer Diess und Jenes erlebt und die Zeichen davon in sein Gedicht hineingeschrieben hatte! — als Dichter waren sie dem antiquarischen Spürgeiste, der dem historischen Sinne voranläuft, abhold, als Dichter liessen sie diese ganz persönlichen Dinge und Namen und Alles, was einer Stadt, einer Küste, einem Jahrhundert als seine Tracht und Maske zu eigen war, nicht gelten, sondern stellten flugs das Gegenwärtige und das Römische an seine Stelle. Sie scheinen uns zu fragen: „Sollen wir das Alte nicht für uns neu machen und uns in ihm zurechtlegen? Sollen wir nicht unsere Seele diesem todten Leibe einblasen dürfen? denn todt ist er nun einmal: wie hässlich ist alles Todte!" — Sie kannten den Genuss des historischen Sinnes nicht; das Vergangene und Fremde war ihnen peinlich, und als Römern ein Anreiz zu einer römischen Eroberung. In der That, man eroberte damals, wenn man übersetzte, — nicht nur so, dass man das Historische wegliess: nein, man fügte die Anspielung auf das Gegenwärtige hinzu, man strich

> vor Allem den Namen des Dichters hinweg und setzte den eigenen an seine Stelle — nicht im Gefühl des Diebstahls, sondern mit dem allerbesten Gewissen des *Imperium Romanum*. (FW §83)

According to the text, although the Romans lacked the historical sense that Nietzsche possessed (he considers himself the first philosopher with a historical sense), they were free-spirited as a nation and they made free-spirited translations of Greek literature. They made the old new, adjusting Greek texts to their time and had no particular interest in keeping Greek ideas fixed and stable. Thus they conquered as they translated, and they did so with a good conscience, without feeling guilty for what they did. Nietzsche praises them for the bravery with which they acted in creating new ideas, which is fundamental to Nietzsche's understanding of Being as (an ever-changing) becoming. For him, being is *becoming,* i.e., reality is in flux and changing, it is unique. To classify reality is to falsify and simplify it.

Becoming for Nietzsche presupposes law-breaking taking place before law-making. He would associate law-breaking with Romans ignoring the individual traits of Greek authors (and replacing their Greek names with Roman names) and the particular characters of the societies they lived in, and law-making with adjustment of Greek originals to Roman standards.

The Romans engaged in free translation because they were not concerned with concepts of truth. Max Stirner was the first to raise the question of the value of truth. "[His] critique of truth as a fixed idea embodied much of what was central to Nietzsche's – the pervasiveness of the will to truth, truth's relationship to divinity, its present existence as an unexamined ideal, and above all its existence as both a symbol and a cause of the inability to enquire and to act freely in all directions." (Bergner 13) In the above-quoted passage on translation, Nietzsche suggests that once Being is viewed as fixed and stable, i.e., as truthful, it begins to suffer the burden of limitations placed upon it. Truth impedes the development of Being, therefore it must necessarily impede the beings of Being, in particular the freedom of translation. Romans were not possessed by concepts of truth as a fixed idea; therefore they acted freely, translating Greek texts as they did.

This is precisely what is lacking in — and what Nietzsche critiques about — Europe, especially the German-speaking people: the sluggishness and pessimism of the Christian *Spannung des Geistes* (JGB Vorrede) spread across Europe. He is raging about the spectre of Schopenhauerian pessimism haunting nineteenth-century Europe. Schopenhauer clearly realised the non-divinity of existence. Yet, according to Nietzsche, he could not answer his own question as to whether existence has any meaning at all.

> ... Die Ungöttlichkeit des Daseins galt ihm (Schopenhauer) als etwas Gegebenes, Greifliches, Undiskutirbares...
> ... [D]as ist nunmehr vorbei, das hat das Gewissen gegen sich, das gilt allen feineren Gewissen als unanständig, unehrlich, als Lügnerei, Femininismus, Schwachheit, Feigheit, — mit dieser Strenge, wenn

irgend womit, sind wir eben gute Europäer und Erben von Europas längster und tapferster Selbstüberwindung. Indem wir die christliche Interpretation dergestalt von uns stossen und ihren „Sinn" wie eine Falschmünzerei verurtheilen, kommt nun sofort auf eine furchtbare Weise die Schopenhauerische Frage zu uns: hat denn das Dasein überhaupt einen Sinn? (FW §357)

Nietzsche explained the event of German (and European) pessimism or nihilism (rejection of everything that is true) as historically positive on the basis of the unconditional honest atheism that had sprung from Christian morality itself after two thousand years' training in truthfulness. He writes:

... der unbedingte redliche Atheismus ist... ein endlich und schwer errungener Sieg des europäischen Gewissens, als der folgenreichste Akt einer zweitausendjährigen Zucht zur Wahrheit, welche am Schlusse sich die Lüge im Glauben an Gott verbietet... Man sieht, was eigentlich über den christlichen Gott gesiegt hat: die christliche Moralität selbst, der immer strenger genommene Begriff der Wahrhaftigkeit, die Beichtväter-Feinheit des christlichen Gewissens, übersetzt und sublimiert zum wissenschaftlichen Gewissen, zur intellektuellen Sauberkeit um jeden Preis. Die Natur ansehn, als ob sie ein Beweis für die Güte und Obhut eines Gottes sei; die Geschichte interpretieren zu Ehren einer göttlichen Vernunft... (FW §357)

Thus now that truth-seeking Christianity has finally found it, it forbids itself the lie involved in the belief of God; Christian morality is overcome, and *das Dasein* has no meaning. Yet, the fact that Nietzsche says that the Germans are not pessimists leaves hope for the opposite idea that they are optimists, and the fact that he also refers to himself as a good European (not a German) calls for a unity not only of *das Volk* but also of *das ganze Europa*. As a good European, Nietzsche writes that

... der Pessimismus Schopenhauers nicht nur ein Ausnahme-Fall unter Deutschen, sondern ein deutsches Ereigniss gewesen ist: während Alles, was sonst im Vordergrunde steht, unsre tapfre Politik, unsre fröhliche Vaterländerei, welche entschlossen genug alle Dinge auf ein wenig philosophisches Princip hin („Deutschland, Deutschland über Alles") betrachtet, also *sub specie speciei,* nämlich der deutschen *species,* mit grosser Deutlichkeit das Gegentheil bezeugt. Nein! die Deutschen von heute sind keine Pessimisten! Und Schopenhauer war Pessimist, nochmals gesagt, als guter Europäer und nicht als Deutscher. — (FW §357)

The Christian conscience translated — and thereby sublimated to the purely intellectual, scientific conscience — experiences a downfall and self-rejection. Only the good Europeans as a whole, who are heirs of Europe's self-overcoming, can realise the non-divine nature of existence and give meaning to their life by creating and living up to their values. The task of Europeans now, as Nietzsche sees it, is to translate the meaningless existence into a fully meaningful *Dasein* that does not mean *being-there* understood as 'being in the world beyond' but *being-here*, i.e., being or living in the present moment of existence as creative individuals on earth. In this context such a translation is synonymous with creation. *Dasein* is translated into *Da-sein*, Being into Be-*ing*, i.e. becoming, with multiple perspectival interpretations thereof, as existing phenomenally, uniquely: Be-*ing* is a creative extension of the origin, a creative translation of the original *to be* into the language of humankind. With such a translation, the human becomes the Overhuman (*Übermensch*). Thus the human being is the self-translator, the translator of his or her own nature originally written in the language of divinity into the mother-tongue of his or her animal nature — and back into divinity — on the basis of bodily participation.

It follows from the above discussion that Nietzsche would want human beings, in particular the Germans, to overcome Christian morality. But what does it mean to be German for Nietzsche, after all? This question can be raised only within the larger context of Nietzsche's conception of translation, which is for him translation of human nature back into its original. Nietzsche recognises that „...der schreckliche Grundtext *homo natura* wieder heraus erkannt werden muss. Den Menschen nämlich zurückübersetzen in die Natur; über die vielen eitlen und schwärmerischen Deutungen und Nebensinne Herr werden, welche bisher über jenen ewigen Grundtext *homo natura* gekritzelt und gemalt wurden..." (JGB §230) For Nietzsche, the translation of humankind back into its nature signifies that human nature is essentially animal nature. It is not merely divine as Christianity has proclaimed it to be. The animal nature of the human being is the original text that has been misinterpreted by Christianity. As a result, a Christian mistranslation of human nature as divine has occurred in the history of Europe, particularly in the history of German-speaking people. It follows that to be human one must become unchristian. If the Germans become unchristian, they become human; if they become human, then they finally become what they are, i.e. German, or good Europeans. It follows that they must become unchristian to be German — this is what is stressed in the concluding quote:

> Vergessen wir doch nicht, dass die Völkernamen gewöhnlich Schimpfnamen sind... Die „Deutschen": das bedeutet urspünglich „die Heiden": so nannten die Gothen nach ihrer Bekehrung die grosse Masse ihrer ungetauften Stammverwandten... Es wäre immer noch möglich, dass die Deutschen aus ihrem alten Schimpfnamen sich nachträglich einen Ehrennamen machten, indem sie das erste unchristliche Volk Europa's würden... (FW §146)

As is clear, Nietzsche does not lose hope that the German-speaking people, although they bear an originally disparaging name *Deutsch*, will unite one day (and they *are* united now: they even constitute the backbone of the European Union – so Nietzsche may be called a prophet) when they shake off one-sided Christian interpretation and engage in perspectivism and phenomenology, in the context of which translation is at the same time necessarily rethought as an aesthetic perspectival interpretation of the original text and reality on the basis of bodily participation.

## Conclusion

In conclusion, the above discussion of Nietzsche's conception of translation has found translation to be a necessary, life-affirming interpretation of both the original text and the reality which both the original and its translation strive to interpret. Furthermore, translation is only an interpretation, to which there can be no alternative. The more translations we make of the same original, the better we are as translators. Perspectival interpretation is the only alternative to methods for accessing truth. Likewise, multiple translations of the original are a wonderful alternative to dogmatically imposing certain rules on translation, thus making only one or few translations of the original possible. It has been shown that the life-invigorating *allegro* element is central to Nietzsche's concept of translation as affirmation and enhancement of existence crucial to the Germans becoming good Europeans within a united Europe.

## Works Cited

Bergner, Jeffrey T. "Stirner, Nietzsche, and the Critique of Truth." *Journal of the History of Philosophy* 11.4 (1973): 523 – 534. *Project Muse*. Web. 19 Nov. 2010.

Nietzsche, Friedrich Wilhelm. *Die fröhliche Wissenschaft*. Leipzig, 1887. http://www.archive.org/stream/completenietasch10nietuoft/completenietasch10nietuoft_djvu.txt. Web. 20 Nov. 2010.

___. *Jenseits von Gut und Böse*. 2005. Web. 19 Nov. 2010. http://www.gutenberg.org/cache/epub/7204/pg7204.txt. Web. 19 Nov. 2010.

___. *Thus Spoke Zarathustra*. *The Portable Nietzsche*. Trans. and ed. Walter Kaufmann. New York: Viking Press, 1968.

___. *On the Genealogy of Morals* in *On the Genealogy of Morals* and *Ecce Homo*. Trans. Walter Kaufmann and R.J. Hollingdale. New York: Vintage Books, 1989.

Robinson, Douglas. Ed. *Western Translation Theory: From Herodotus to Nietzsche*. Manchester: St. Jerome Publishing, 1997.

Schrift, Alan D. "Language, Metaphor, Rhetoric: Nietzsche's Deconstruction of Epistemology." *Journal of the History of Philosophy* 23.3 (1985): 371 – 395. *Project Muse*. Web. 19 Nov. 2010.

# Nietzsche's Interpretation of the Bible
(2009)

## Introduction

The purpose of this research is to examine Nietzsche's interpretation of the Bible. Anti-Semitic issues connected to Nietzsche's critique of Christianity and Judaism will be touched upon first. For it is in the anti-Semitic environment of nineteenth-century Europe that Nietzsche lived and worked. *The Antichrist* was partly Nietzsche's response to anti-Semitism, which provides us with an opportunity to look at his unique biblical exegesis.

Isaiah and Paul are the two major figures in Nietzsche's interpretation. Isaiah's prophecies of the coming of the Messiah (who would restore peace in Israel), reinforced by his vivid imagination, get caught up in Paul's messianic interpretation that, according to Nietzsche, stems from resentment against the Jewish Law. This leads to the falsification of the figure of Jesus Christ. Christian revenge for the crucifixion blots out Jesus' peacefulness and non-resistance to evil. My view is that Nietzsche attempts to exonerate both Christians and Jews from all possible "sin" that they attribute to one another in their Jewish-Christian polemics as to the coming of the Messiah. I argue that for Nietzsche, the Messiah has not come unless he has come with genuine Christianity. For the purpose of establishing what is meant by genuine Christianity, it is necessary to examine Nietzsche's critique of both the Old and the New Testaments and see what stands between them, at the juncture of the Jewish and Christian polemics.

I shall come to the conclusion that Paul's resentment and faith woven into the resurrection of Jesus falsified the original symbolism of the figure of Christ. As a result, the Messiah has not come unless he has come in his original state (as Nietzsche viewed it), perhaps not as Isaiah imagined and not as ancient Jews anticipated, whose tradition yet produced the Saviour.

## 2. Judaism vs. Christianity

Walter Kaufman duly notes that Nietzsche may seem at first glance an anti-Semite but, if one takes a closer look, one will discover "that Nietzsche is as opposed to anti-Semitism as ever." (Santaniello 163) In the nineteenth century, Christian anti-Semites degraded both original Israel and contemporary Jewry, while at the same time claiming that the priestly Judaism prophesied Jesus as the Messiah. Nietzsche is bold enough to overturn this position. He supports original Israel and contemporary Jewry and ascribes "Judeo-Christianity" to *ressentiment*, the French word for resentment, revenge, that Christians take against everything Jewish. In *The Antichrist*, Nietzsche "elevates ancient Hebrews and modern Jews, but he is ambivalent toward prophetic-priestly Judaism, which he believes gave rise to (false) Christianity." (Santaniello164)

Nietzsche understands Christianity "as the religion of mass *ressentiment*" (Santaniello 166) and attempts to reverse the position of the traditional Christian anti-Semitism of his time. One has to closely evaluate Nietzsche's texts that deal with Judaism and the Jews and how the latter are related to Christianity. *The Antichrist* is central in understanding the distinction between the Old and New Testaments. Nietzsche's infamous words from the *Genealogy of Morals*: "With the Jews there begins *the slave revolt in morality*...." (Nietzsche GM, I, 7), if taken out of context, may lead one to believe that he is an anti-Semite. One has to hear Nietzsche's complete sentence. In reality Nietzsche makes reference to the Jews of early Christian times, the so-called "Christian-Jews." Nietzsche actually attacks Christian, not Jewish, morality "— that revolt which has a history of two thousand years behind it, and which we no longer see because it — has been victorious." (Nietzsche GM, I, 7) In *The Antichrist*, he is against anti-Semitism, opposing all kinds of demeanour of both original Israel and contemporary Jewry, "locating the spiritual development of Christianity within the priestly-prophetic strand of Judaism, especially that of the prophet Isaiah." (Santaniello 167)

Nietzsche concedes the fact "that Christianity originated with the prophet Isaiah," yet "he disagrees that this represents spiritual *progress*, but rather, the origin of *Israel's* demise, which has culminated in the (anti-Semitic) Christianity of *ressentiment*." (Santaniello 169) What Nietzsche does is elevate the ancient Yahweh over the Christian God:

> How can anyone today still submit to the simplicity of Christian theologians to the point of insisting with them that the development of the conception of God from the "God of Israel," the god of a people, to the Christian God, the quintessence of everything good,

represents *progress*?... After all, the opposite stares you in the face. When the presuppositions of *ascending* life, when everything strong, brave, masterful, and proud is eliminated from the conception of God . . . and the attribute "Savior" or "Redeemer" remains in the end as the one essential attribute of divinity — just *what* does such a transformation signify? what, such a *reduction* of the divine? (A 17)

Nietzsche opposes any preference for the Christian God to that of the powerful Yahweh: "I am against any attempt to introduce the fanatic into the Redeemer type... The 'glad tidings' are precisely that there are no longer any opposites; the kingdom of heaven belongs to the children... Such a faith is not angry, does not reproach, does not resist; it does not bring "the sword." (A 32) For Nietzsche, the Christian God is "one of the most corrupt conceptions of the divine ever attained on earth." (A 18) "Almost two thousand years," Nietzsche writes, "and not a single new god!" (A 19) For him, the Jews are the antithesis of all decadents and a people endowed with the toughest vitality. Nietzsche sharply distinguishes between ancient Jews, "Christian Jews," and modern Jews. He writes:

> The Christian church cannot make the slightest claim to originality when compared with the "holy people." That precisely is why the Jews are the most catastrophic people of world history; by their aftereffect they have made mankind so thoroughly false that even today the Christian can feel anti-Jewish

without realizing that he himself is *the ultimate Jewish consequence.* (A 24)

Psychologically considered, the Jewish people are a people endowed with the toughest vital energy, who, placed in impossible circumstances . . . divined a power in these instincts with which one could prevail against "the world." The Jews are the antithesis of all decadents: they had to represent decadents to the point of illusion; with a *non plus ultra* of histrionic genius they have known how to place themselves at the head of all movements of decadents (as Pauline Christianity). (A 24)

Nietzsche views Christianity as born out of the priestly Judaism. The priestly element that exists within Judaism and Christianity is utterly responsible for the decadence of Christianity. The God of Power is the God of original Israel: "Yahweh is the God of Israel and therefore the god of justice; the logic of every people that is in power and has a good conscience." (A 25) Beginning with Isaiah the God of Judgement is associated with Judea and Christianity. The God of resentment is considered as the "good" God. The good God is sentimentally represented by Jesus Christ and at the same time by the vengeful God as created by Isaiah and Paul. Yahweh, originally a "God of justice", who signified the "self-affirmation" and "self-confidence" of a people and "was the expression of a consciousness of power, of joy in oneself, of hope for oneself" (A 25), began to denature with the Hebrew prophets, such as Isaiah. Isaiah began interpreting events of natural causality in terms of reward and punishment. With this taking place, morality was detached from the instincts that would otherwise play an important role in the preservation and enhancement of life.

In *The Antichrist*, Nietzsche addresses the notion of the Last Judgement. The early Christian community "created its god according to its needs and put words into its Master's mouth," hence "those wholly unevangelical concepts it now cannot do without: the return, the 'Last Judgment,' every kind of temporal expectation and promise." (A 31) To the newly created God of Judgement were ascribed the notions of punishment and reward. The principle of obedience and disobedience to the will of God was conducive to the concept of sin that became a tool in the hands of vengeful priests, who oppressed and controlled society. "All natural occurrences, such as birth, marriage, death, and sickness were 'denatured' in order to make the priest indispensable. The severed natural realm, which was formerly intertwined with the conception of Yahweh, now first had to be consecrated by the priest in order to be rendered holy." (Santaniello 171) Out of this false soil Christianity grew up.

Thus, for Nietzsche, Isaiah was the turning point in the history of Israel. The prophet is at the juncture between the life-affirming Judaism and the decadent Christianity. But the question "Who is to blame for the rise of the decadent Christianity out of the decaying priestly-prophetic Judaism — the Yahweh Jews or the Christian Jews?" must remain rhetorical for two reasons. First, the Christian Jews project their one true Christian God but at the same time they deny the "holy" and "chosen" people of Israel and all Jewish reality, on which it was based. Second, the Yahweh Jews do not recognise the coming of Messiah, remaining faithful to their Judaism, the priestly decadence of which gave rise to Christianity, and forget that it is precisely natural tribulations of those times that led Isaiah to prophesy the coming of a person who would liberate the land of Israel from possible war tensions and restore peace.

In tracing anti-Semitism from the rise of the Christian church to his contemporaries, such as Renan and Dühring, who were two of the most vicious anti-Semites in nineteenth century-Europe, Nietzsche finds that anti-Semites, while locating the origin of Christianity with the prophet Isaiah, cut off original Israel and contemporary Jews. They did so by using the words of Isaiah: " 'Hear, indeed, but do not understand; see, indeed, but do not grasp.' Dull that people's mind" (*The Jewish Study Bible*, Isa. 6:9-10) *against* German Jews because the latter rejected salvation and the Saviour, Jesus Christ. We find Isaiah quoted and used against the Jews in the New Testament (Mk 4:12; Acts 28:26). Because Israel rejected salvation in Christ, they were denied that 'salvation.' "[T]his salvation of God has been sent to the Gentiles," Paul says, "they will listen." (*The New Oxford Annotated Bible*, Acts 28:28) Nietzsche may seem to be attacking Judaism and the prophet Isaiah but he is actually anti-anti-Semitic. Moreover, Nietzsche writes: "In Christianity, all of Judaism . . . attains its ultimate mastery as the art of lying in a holy manner. The Christian, the *ultima ratio* of the lie, is the Jew once more — even *three* times more." (A 44) "If we have even the smallest claim to integrity, we must know today that a theologian, a priest, a pope, not merely is wrong in every sentence he speaks, but lies —"

(A 38) Nietzsche continues to say that everybody knows this "*but everything continues as before.*" (A 38)

Finally, Nietzsche makes a distinction between the corrupt traditional understanding of Jesus and the historical Jesus: "There was only *one* Christian, and he died on the cross." (A 39) For Nietzsche, the New Testament remains valuable as "evidence of corruption *within* the first community" (A 44). At the end of *The Antichrist*, Nietzsche pronounces his judgement: he condemns Christianity and laments that time is reckoned after "this calamity began — after the *first* day of Christianity. Why not rather after its last day! After today? Revaluation of all values!" (A 62)

We can conclude from this section that, according to Nietzsche, the priestly Judaism coexisting with the original Yahweh was decadent enough to produce a prophecy of the Messiah whose interpretation was later corrupted by resentful Christian Jews. As a result, we have the false Messiah "saving the world." Let us further examine what lies at the core of such Messianic fabrication.

## 3. Nietzsche contra Paul

According to Nietzsche, Christianity falsely interprets "all history prior to Jesus as a foreshadowing of Christ's coming." (Millen 104) It falsifies the future with "eternal life," and all reality, for God is not static and unchanging. On the contrary, life is an eternal process of creative becoming. Nietzsche's critique of Christianity is primarily concerned with the Christian concept of morality, eschatology, and the figure of Christ as the Redeemer.

"The vitality of human creativity requires not the timidity, pity, and humility praised as Christian values, but courage, honesty, and genuine searchings that lead toward the flourishing of life, not the glorification of death." (Millen 104–105) Mere faith or blind faith takes one nowhere. In contrast, Jewish tradition has always stressed deed over creed.

Whereas Jewish tradition tries to balance communal with individual needs, thus not following the flock (with a herd mentality as the basis of a community), the Christian emphasis on a community of believers subservient to the Redeemer and the Church is contradictory to its own focus on one's individual salvation. The Jewish redemption is not an individual salvation; but a just society must be created as a prerequisite for salvation. Jewish tradition redeems the community together with the individual. The Hebrew Bible sometimes seems to Nietzsche to be even superior to the Greek Bible.

But he is ambivalent in respect to the Greek Bible. On the one hand, it is a falsification of the Hebrew Bible; on the other, it records the greatest *will to power* (and to overpower others) exercised by ancient Christian Jews, which, according to Nietzsche, defines human nature as such. He praises Jewish culture, full as it is of vital energy. Yet he holds the priestly type of Judaism responsible for the slave morality so characteristic of Christian society. Jewish values affirmed both noble goodness and that which was weak and poor. These were inherited by Christianity, and the priests of ancient Israel and the medieval church sought to exercise power over the sick flock. So, ancient Israel is the source of resentment, the

Christian slave morality. But at the same time the original Israel represents, for Nietzsche, spiritual strength and power. In contrast, the spiritual strength of Christianity is based on denigration of the Jews. Nietzsche blames Paul for his resentment against the Jewish Law. Nietzsche's scathing critique of Paul's teachings does not suggest that he admires Paul in any way. But it would be fair to assert that at times Nietzsche is indeed fascinated by him, for he feels helpless at Paul's having skilfully posited truth as falsehood.

We know that Paul quotes the *Book of Isaiah* most often and he makes use of the Psalms too. Paul reads the Old Testament as the prophecy of the messianic salvation. He preaches either as a missionary or directly to established congregations. For Paul, Christianity, as we know it today, is "messianically completed Judaism." (Hübner 341) According to Hans Hübner, for Paul, the justification occurs through faith alone, not by fulfilling the law. Paul seems not to deny but to expand the original meaning of the Old Testament. The turning point in Paul's interpretation of the Jewish Law is as follows: everyone "is cursed who does not obey *everything* written in the book of the law." (Hübner 342) Since no one obeys the law, everyone is under a curse and must seek salvation (Deut. 27:26). Thus Paul gives a new reading of the law, a new self-understanding.

There is a theological domination involved in Paul's interpretation of the Old Testament. The law is the word of promise of personal salvation and one must now fulfil only one commandment: love your neighbour. Paul reads Isaiah as follows: God "wants salvation for all of Israel." (Hübner

345) But when does this salvation occur — today? tomorrow? or never? For Paul, it is "the event of the last day," whereas for Ezekiel, it is in the course of history alone that the "spiritual restoration of all Israel" (Hübner 347) must take place.

In light of the above, I think that for Nietzsche, Paul's imposition of the messianic salvation upon Israel is another form of morality that seeks to control ancient Israelites. Nietzsche takes issue not only with Pauline Christianity but with the whole of Christian morality. For Nietzsche, the entire Bible is permeated with morality, beginning with the creation of the world, when God tells Adam to labour and sweat and Eve to bear children in pain. The question of the coming of the Messiah is intricately bound up with Christian morality. According to Nietzsche, the fact that the Messiah sacrifices himself does not bring life into the world, for one must sacrifice external commands (Thou shalt) and become an internal commander (I will) and thus overcome one's sinful nature and be able to create new values. Until then, the Messiah has not come.

However, David Weiss Halivni reminds us that the laws given in the Old Testament are "self-evident;" there are "justified laws." (9) But if reasons are given, it will "induce people to draw the wrong conclusions." (10) Motive clauses such as "for," "therefore," "lest," etc. explain the reasons for which the law is given. To take an example, Deuteronomy has the largest number of motive clauses, whereas the Cultic Decalogue has the smallest number. The two major reasons for morality are the creation and the redemption themes (freeing from slavery, i.e. the exodus from Egypt), which leads to the creation of the covenant. In my judgement, Jews, while being delivered from the bondage of slavery, immediately pass into the bondage of moral obedience to the Lord. Since "the motive clause appeals to logic," while "the exegetical motive appeals to authority" according to Halivni (15), morality, in my view, becomes entrenched in both logic and authority. I think that for Nietzsche, authoritative morality coupled with Paul's logic prevails and thus breeds the slave Christian morality of the herd. Although Midrash provides authority for interpretation and guides exegetes by the formula "as it is written," it still falls prey to slave morality for Nietzsche. One remains bound by the moral rules. Morality makes one's interpretations blind. The plain sense of things is confused with their metaphorical, moral interpretation; therefore, the motivations that stand behind those things remain hidden and unexamined. Nietzsche attempts to investigate the hiddenness of Paul's interpretation of the Old Testament.

According to Frank Kermode, modern interpretations of the Bible find the plain sense in the here and now rather than in the origin of the text. Modernists strive to close the gap between doctrine and text by new interpretations. (190) This is due to the fact that the plain sense of things changes with interpretation through time. And what is an interpretation if not a metaphor? Hence "metaphor runs in the world's blood." (Kermode 192)

Interpretation is always a metaphoric imagination which will never allow for a plain sense, precisely because it must not allow. (Kermode 193) In this respect, Nietzsche sees Paul's interpretation not only as moralistic but also highly metaphorical, which leads to the ephemeral symbolism of the Redeemer. My view is that Nietzsche's interpretation of the Bible, particularly of Pauline Christianity, is that of a psychologist. He skilfully delves into Paul's state of mind and searches for the motivations that stand behind Paul's actions. Paul's resentment against the old law is the work of his instinct of self-preservation conducive to his invention of such symbolic notions as Resurrection, Redemption, Judgement and the Beyond.

The problem of Paul is a very complex one. In his first major book *Paul and Palestinian Judaism*, E.P. Sanders argued that the traditional Christian interpretation of Paul as being against Rabbinic legalism misunderstood both Judaism and Paul's thought. One had to abide by God's covenant with Abraham and one remained bound by the covenant by keeping the Law. Sanders argued that Paul's faith in Christ was the only means of becoming one of the People of God and the old covenant played no sufficient role in it. But, in order to stay in, one had to keep some aspects of the Jewish Law. Paul did not insist on faith in Christ as the only means of being admitted to God's grace. Sanders emphasised Paul's love of good deeds. So, there was and is a necessity for good works in addition to mere faith in Christ. In my judgement, however, keeping some aspects of the law is not keeping all of them. Also, the new covenant presupposes the new God even if faith in Christ is supported by good works. Still, Nietzsche holds Paul's invention of personal immortality through faith in the resurrection of Christ accountable for indoctrinating unreality in herd mentality.

For Nietzsche, the case of Paul is the case against Christianity. Nietzsche sees him "as the prototypical ascetic priest so reviled" (Acampora 34) in *On the Genealogy of Morals*. In his article "Nietzsche Contra Homer, Socrates, and Paul," Christa D. Acampora considers the two facets of the issue of Paul: "*Saul*'s conversion and *Paul*'s exegesis." Nietzsche clearly sees "Paul as the inventor of Christianity — as the revaluator of the symbol of Jesus." (Acampora 34) For Nietzsche, Saul metamorphoses to Paul. Paul creates values that inhibit "the production of [the] alternative values... that might contest the Christian/ascetic ideal." (Acampora 35) In *Daybreak* § 68, Nietzsche writes that Saul "was constantly combating and on the watch for transgressors and doubters, harsh and malicious towards them and with the extremest inclination for punishment." But later on, Paul himself realises that even he is unable to fulfil all the requirements of the law. What drives Paul for Nietzsche is his thirst to subdue and overpower others. Paul begins to despise the whole institution responsible for the crucifixion of Jesus: "The law was the cross to which he felt himself nailed: how he hated it! How he had to drag it along! How he sought about for a means of *destroying* it." Paul manages to find the means of destroying it in the figure of Christ and "*Saul becomes Paul* as he conspires to secure his freedom from the law." (Acampora 35) He overturns the law. Paul is not a rebel against the law and he seeks to free himself not from the obligations of the law but from the tyrannical institutions that enforce it. "[T]he law existed so that sins might be committed, it continually brought sin forth..." (Acampora 35) The impossibility of fulfilling the law makes Saul's life sinful, therefore worthless. Jesus Christ is dead to evil — so the law that determines sin dies, Nietzsche explains:

> Even if it is still possible to sin, it is no longer possible to sin against the law… God could never have resolved on the death of Christ if a fulfillment of the law had been in any way possible without this death; now not only has all guilt been taken away, guilt as such has been destroyed; now the law is dead, now the carnality in which it dwelt is dead. (Acampora 36)

In place of the law, Paul, now liberated from its slavery but at the same time feeling the urge to fill the void and be distinguished, erects another ideal. He takes revenge against "the injustice of the *end* of Jesus' life" and concentrates on "what it means to struggle and fight in the wake of that event." (Acampora 36) But the original symbol of the figure of Christ is that he never resists evil, he is free from resentment. Nietzsche here distinguishes between Christian dogmatic teachings and the life of Jesus Christ: "in truth, there was only *one* Christian, and he died on the cross. The 'evangel' *died* on the cross. What has been called 'evangel' from that moment was actually the opposite of that which *he* had lived: '*ill* tidings,' a *dysangel*." (A 39) The Christ ideal as created by Paul is an utter "transmogrification of Nietzsche's Jesus." (Acampora 36) Jesus, or the Messiah, lives and dies freely; he is free from the limitations of "any kind of word, formula, law, faith, dogma": "the whole of reality, the whole of nature, language itself, has for him only the value of a sign, a simile" (A 32). Jesus is a symbolist *par excellence* (A 34).

For Nietzsche, the miracle worker and Redeemer are nothing but ephemeral symbolism. Beginning with the death on the cross, the history of Christianity is the history of the misunderstanding of an original symbolism, in which the Messiah could possibly exist. The original symbolism (A 37) is blessedness and perfection (A 34) achieved by affirmation of existence, in unity with the world, where the concept of sin and guilt is abolished and the "cleavage between God and man" is obliterated. (A 41) "Jesus is thought to *live out* this unity as an affirmation much like the Israelites Nietzsche admires in his account of the early history of Judaism (A 25). (Acampora 36) Thus, once Jesus is thought of as affirmation of life, he is inevitably the Messiah in Nietzsche's view.

The "rebellion against the existing order" (A 40) seeks to lay blame for Jesus' death. It is permeated with resentment. The desire for revenge culminates in the creation of the symbol of the Redeemer as struggling. Jesus' life is distanced, separated, from the practice of living. Paul introduces the dogma of salvation through faith, absolute belief, in the doctrine of resurrection that brings about this separation. Nietzsche sees Paul's whole conception of Christianity in the following sentence: "If Christ has not been raised (from the dead), then our proclamation has been in vain and your faith has been in vain." (*The New Oxford Annotated Bible*, I Corinthians 15:14)

Furthermore, the human life of Jesus does not have any value for Paul. Absolute faith in the resurrection of the body of Christ denies human experience. Everything is in vain, if the resurrection did not happen. Thus Paul, when he "places life's center of gravity not in life but in the 'beyond' — *in nothingness* — [he] deprives life of its center of gravity altogether." (A 43) Jesus, when elevated to a supernatural status, simply fails as a model for human emulation. Thus He comes to represent retribution for injustice: "Precisely the most unevangelical feeling, *revenge*, came to the fore again. The matter could not possibly be finished with this death: 'retribution' was needed, 'judgment' (and yet, what could possibly be more unevangelical than 'retribution,' 'punishment,' 'sitting in judgment'!)" (A 40) It follows that such a Messiah is detached from reality, hence non-existent, hence he has not come.

Paul's revaluation of values is nothing but a disaster; it renders humanity decadent through the false notions mentioned above. In § 85 of *Human All Too Human* II [2], Nietzsche writes that Paul remains Saul, a persecutor of God. Paul's invention of Christianity is rooted in the destructive aim of Saul's rebellion. The belief that Paul propagates, however, must be woven into one's practices (which Paul may not deny, as according to E.P. Sanders). Yet Nietzsche's point is this, that Christians have never had such belief, if one is to understand Christianity in its proper sense, and never lived a life modelled on that of Jesus Christ, the Messiah. In other words, Nietzsche understands Christianity as a way of life, not as a way of belief per se. Nietzsche's central criticism of Pauline Christianity consists in this, that the substitution of the belief in the redemption through Jesus Christ for a way of life as lived by him who died on the cross has perverted the whole notion of genuine Christianity. As Nietzsche himself put it:

> From now on there is introduced into the type of the redeemer step by step: the doctrine of a Judgement and a Second Coming, the doctrine of his death as a sacrificial death, the doctrine of the Resurrection with which the entire concept 'blessedness,' the whole and sole reality of the Evangel, is juggled away for the benefit of a state *after* death! Paul with that rabbinical insolence which characterises him in every respect, rationalised this interpretation, this *indecency* of an interpretation, thus: '*If* Christ is not resurrected from the dead our faith is in vain.' All at once the Evangel became the most contemptible of all unfulfillable promises, the *impudent* doctrine of personal immortality... Paul himself even taught it as a *reward*!... (A 41)

It is clear that Paul's Messiah, in Nietzsche's view, has not made even the slightest attempt at his own arrival but is still being promised and prophesied, if not by Isaiah and not even by Paul, then by Pauline Christians.

Nietzsche's reference to *I Corinthians 15* in which Paul proclaims that "[i]f the dead are not raised," then all that is left is "[l]et us eat and drink, for tomorrow we die," seeks to make this point, that the following set of beliefs: "belief in a free willing subject, belief in a God of judgement and belief in immortality of the soul... become substituted for Christ's way of living and, as such, lead to another way of living in which the profession and manifestation of faith is central." (Owen 36) Such empty faith only mesmerises individuals and makes them "true" Christians in the sense of Pauline Christianity, no matter how much emphasis Paul may have made on deeds.

The above is confirmed by Nietzsche in the story of the Madman who one morning lit a lantern and went out in search of God, shouting: "I am looking for God! I am looking for God," and asking the passers-by where the almighty one had gone. The urban atheists to whom the madman speaks are "true" Christians, Christians as shaped by Paul's mere set of beliefs. They "remain all-too-Christian in that they are held captive by... psychological self-misunderstanding exhibited by Pauline Christianity." (Owen 36)

For Nietzsche, Paul is the real creator of ascetic ideals: "Paul simply shifted the centre of gravity of that entire existence [as demonstrated by the life and death of the Evangel] *beyond* this existence in the *lie* of the 'resurrected' Jesus." (A 42) Hence, the false notions of belief as described above come into play and start to manipulate and control the believers. Nietzsche's keen psychological insight into the text written by Paul discloses the sharp contrast between Christ himself as an example of practised peace and tranquility reinforced by self-reflexivity and the symbolic, ephemeral ideal of Christ as created by Paul, as the one who is miraculously resurrected from the dead and is to return to judge and punish the unfaithful.

## Conclusion

In closing, Paul simply denies all possible *human* existence to Jesus as a person, as an individual, nails Him with his doctrines to the cross in the hearts of the herd of stupefied believers and proclaims Him as the only true goal to which humanity should strive — all to attain personal immortality in the world beyond, away from all reality and human, down-to-earth achievements. The promise of life after death and other "rewards" that Paul teaches now become the sole reality in which the Christian believer envisions him- or herself as existing. This promised and anticipated existence, or rather non-existence, that is beyond the real world, does not effect the fulfilment of the promise of real existence in the real world: the coming of the Messiah in peaceful, self-reflexive co-existence with one's neighbour as the manifestation of love of humanity.

We have seen that Nietzsche, by responding to the anti-Semitism of his time, provides a scathing critique of both Christianity and Judaism. He holds Paul responsible for exercising resentment against the Jewish God or law, which led to the creation of such false Christian notions as salvation, judgement, punishment, life in the beyond and faith as based on those false notions. This is plainly a falsification of Christianity. As a result, the Messiah, even if he was prophesied by Isaiah, as Christians interpret, and may not be the Saviour for Jews, who do not recognise the Messiah as the liberator from war, must not have come for certain unless he has come in the original symbolism of Jesus Christ — peace and non-resistance to evil (as

Nietzsche saw it), harmony in unity with the world and love of one's neighbour, where all "sin" is abolished.

## Works Cited

Acampora, Christa Davis. "Nietzsche Contra Homer, Socrates, and Paul" *Journal of Nietzsche Studies*, (#24, 2002): 25 – 53.

Halivni, David Weiss. *Midrash, Mishnah and Gemara: The Jewish Predilection for Justified Law*, Cambridge: Harvard University Press, 1986.

Hübner, Hans. "New Testament Interpretation of the Old Testament" (332 – 372), *Hebrew Bible / Old Testament: The History of its Interpretation* ed. Saebo, Göttingen: Vandenhoeck & Ruprecht, 1996.

Kermode, Frank. "The Plain Sense of Things" *Midrash and Literature* ed. G.H. Hartman and S. Budick, Yale University Press, 1986.

Millen, Rochelle L. Review: Weaver Santaniello, *Nietzsche, God, and The Jews: His Critique of Judeo-Christianity in Relation to the Nazi Myth*. Albany: SUNY Press, 1994, 214 pp. in *Modern Judaism* (#17.1, 1997): 97-104.

Nietzsche, Friedrich. *The Antichrist* in *The Portable Nietzsche*, tr. Walter Kaufmann, New York: The Viking Press, 1954.

\_\_\_. *On the Genealogy of Morals* in *On the Genealogy of Morals*, *Ecce Homo* and *Daybreak* tr. Walter Kaufmann and R.J. Hollingdale, New York: Vintage Books, Inc., 1989.

Owen, David. "Nietzsche's Event: Genealogy and the Death of God" The Johns Hopkins University Press: 2003.

Santaniello, Weaver. "Nietzsche's *Antichrist*: 19th-Century Christian Jews and the Real 'Big Lie' " *Modern Judaism* (#17.2, 1997): 163-177.

# Love of Neighbour
# in Nietzsche's Philosophy
## (2010)

### Introduction

This research explores the true meaning of love of neighbour as based on what Friedrich Nietzsche calls *intellectual honesty* or *conscience*. (*The Gay Science* #2) Intellectual honesty, our last virtue now that the belief in God is dead (GS #343), is the kernel of the self-reflexive ascetic ideal that conquers the unreflexive ascetic ideal and thus affirms creative, self-loving existence. With that in mind, I take a psychological-theological approach toward understanding and researching the relationship between human beings and argue that love of neighbour is primarily love of oneself.

The present research will draw mainly on Nietzsche's *On the Genealogy of Morals* (GM), *The Gay Science* (GS), *Thus Spoke Zarathustra* (TSZ) and *Beyond Good and Evil* (BGE) — together with selected passages from the Bible — to show that what Nietzsche calls the ascetic ideal being turned against itself, being bent inward, (although it has played the only role in the spiritual development of humankind), was in its bending outward precisely the opposite of what I shall examine as Christ's incapacity for physical resistance as love of neighbour through self-reflexivity as perspectivism. Yet, now that the ascetic ideal (the spiritual will to truth at any price, as I understand it) finally has become conscious of itself (GM 27), there is a need on the part of the morally responsible human being to reinterpret *love of neighbour* as *love of oneself*, as Christ's incapacity for physical resistance against others must have implied. This will help explain Christ's unconditional love of humanity as the state of mind of an Overman who embraces life, good and evil, by willing the past to return to the present from the future.

A morally responsible and self-reflexive individual is capable of loving him- or herself and the neighbour on the basis of having overcome his or her ascetic ideal and discharged his or her instincts through spirituality, by embracing and affirming life in every moment of existence. Nietzsche's literary character Zarathustra (TSZ) does conquer his ascetic ideal in the eternal return of the same events (GM 24; TSZ "On Redemption" and "On the Vision and the Riddle").

It seems to me that there may be a parallel drawn between Zarathustra and Christ. Christ, too, in my mind, conquers his ascetic ideal. Christ's incapacity for physical resistance against others as love of neighbour, which paradoxically stems from his having conquered his ascetic ideal, will be placed within the context of Nietzsche's idea of the eternal return to show that, because of Christ's different perception of time, he is capable of living not only in the present and the past but also in the future.

## 2. Christ, the Overman, Eternal Return

Creativity is possible only on the basis of the ascetic ideal. This means, in simple words, that the human being cannot create anything unless he or she tyrannises him- or herself. The human being can be liberated from self-tyranny only if he or she creates. An eternal self-tyranny presupposes an eternal creativity, that is, an eternal interpretation of the world, of one's relationship to the world and the neighbour. It seems to me that Christ's interpretation of the world as unconditional love of humanity is his interpretation of his relation to himself and others, it is not without self-tyranny. But does this kind of interpretation presuppose a clearly defined contrast between the false and the true, or does Christ mean by *truth* various shades or degrees of the apparent world, the world of ideas, in Nietzsche's sense? (BGE #34) When Christ says that he is the truth and Pilate asks what truth is, Christ gives no answer because, it seems to me, truth is not clearly defined, but it is fluid. But there is something that stands behind this fluidity: intellectual honesty armed with the evangelical sword that Christ brings to the world (e.g., the cursing of the barren fig tree). Christ searches for truth not because he does not have it, but precisely because he has found it: honesty with himself. His search for truth does not presuppose simply doing good (to one's neighbour) in the sense that Nietzsche critiques Voltair's maxim: "*il ne cherche le vrai que pour faire le bien*" (BGE # 35) (one searches for truth only to do good), but there is, of course, room here for the evangelical sword. Christ wields it against himself and overcomes his self-tyranny through spiritual creativity.

Moreover, Christ's love of humankind is an *active force*, which, in Nietzsche's language, can be called the Will to Power (BGE #36). His love as the will to power is the cause of itself. His love interprets the world and is interpreted by its own interpretation. Christ's love as the will to power does not disprove God (he says that he has come not to abolish the Law but to fulfil it); on the contrary, it affirms the divinity of the human being. As Nietzsche would say, one does not deny God if one defines God as the will to power (BGE #35), as an interpretation of the world.

Christ's love is profound and it has been wearing a mask. The mask has been placed upon it by idolatrous Christianity. As Nietzsche put it, every profound spirit needs a mask; the profound spirit is falsified by a superficial interpretation of its words and actions. (BGE 40)

In light of the above, the commanded morality of 'love your neighbour as yourself' — in Nietzsche's language "you shall" — must be replaced by the morality one commands to oneself, that is, by "I will." Such replacement can take place only in the eternal return of the same events. The eternal return is such a state of mind where one wills to experience all of his or her past events, both good and evil, all over again. According to Nietzsche, humankind has made its way from the worm to the ape, from the ape to the human being, and now humankind has to make its way to the Overman. (TSZ Prologue) What is at issue here is the perception of time by the consciousness. Animals live only in the present (from the viewpoint of the human being who lives in the present and the past); humans live in the present and the past (from the viewpoint of a human who lives in the present, past and future); whereas Nietzsche's literary character Zarathustra can also "live *even in his future*" (Loeb 89), because he is the conqueror of the eternal return. Such a conqueror of the eternal return is the Overman, because he *overcomes* time and all events, good and evil, within it.

The conqueror of the eternal return overcomes time when his or her will, frustrated at being unable to change the past, turns to the eternal return in order to will it. (TSZ "On Redemption") The will is possessed by *the spirit of revenge* against the past: "the will's ill will against time and its 'it was'" is what Zarathustra calls revenge. (TSZ 252) The will takes revenge against the past because it cannot will backwards. "The will cannot will backwards; and that he (the will) cannot break time and time's covetousness, that is the will's loneliest melancholy." (TSZ 251) The vengeful will wills the past to pass, and in doing so, it wills itself to pass. The will must redeem itself from its revenge. "*That man be delivered from revenge*, that is for me the bridge to the highest hope, and a rainbow after long storms," Zarathustra says in "On the Tarantulas" (TSZ 211). In order to be delivered from revenge – and "[w]illing liberates" (TSZ 251) – the will must learn to will backwards. "Who could teach him (the will) also to will backwards?" (TSZ 253) The will itself should do so: "To redeem those who lived in the past and to recreate all 'it was' into a 'thus I willed it' – that alone I call redemption" (TSZ 251), says Zarathustra. Thus, in willing the past, the will wills itself, it liberates itself from the spirit of revenge against the past, and the past is redeemed through the present at every moment. Instinct and reason should merge into one whole at every creative moment of existence: thus the unreflexive, instinctive aspect of the ascetic ideal becomes one with the self-reflexive aspect of the ascetic ideal.

For the Overman, evil, guilt, regrets, pains etc. are not in the past but are coming in the eternal return. The formula for this eternal return would be: I will and shall will all of it – thus speaks Zarathustra. Zarathustra's own self wills his own self, good and evil, thus liberating his imprisoned will from the past. In this sense, there is an eternal return to oneself, and the ascetic ideal is redirected from the inside outward. The instincts are discharged not as evil but as good, in the form of creativity: art, science and philosophy, thereby at the same time holding a sort of check on the evil forces within, not suppressing them but making use of them as fuel for a passionate relation toward Being through love as meaning, given to the whole of existence. Now the formula 'I will and shall will all of it' becomes 'I love and shall love all of them.' Such would be Christ's love, and for him there was no escape from the eternal return once he entered the spiritual circle of existence.

The main basis for this research is the principle of love of neighbour being love of oneself, which involves the revaluation of the three major concepts in the very principle itself: each of these, namely love, neighbour and self, must be questioned against themselves. Love, for example, emerges, as to conquer it, where there is hatred, paradoxically being a helpful tool in rethinking one's relation to the neighbour. The neighbour is always next to us, always around the corner, or inconceivably far away, and could turn out to be our worst enemy for our own benefit. The self, however, may prove to be selfish, if it fails to be perspectively self-reflexive, or turn against itself to critique itself, its own hatred, on the basis of love; thus becoming the worst enemy to its former self-friendship while at the same time speaking the language of love to its own existence. The self and the neighbour are both friends and enemies to themselves, and so are they to each other. But the relation of the self to the neighbour is inevitably dependent on the relation of the self to its own self. If the self hates itself, and leaves itself with its hatred alone, then it also hates the neighbour. If, on the other hand, the self loves itself, its own hatred, has control over it and uses it towards self-reflexive spirituality, then it loves the other. In short, if the self is not its own neighbour, then there is no neighbour at all. Our last virtue, as Nietzsche calls it, is *intellectual honesty*, which is rooted in Christianity. This virtue is the basis for establishing a loving relationship with ourselves and our neighbours, and this is Christ's truth.

The latter love reaches its pinnacle in the case only of the Overman being able to love humanity unconditionally. Unconditional love of humanity, as Nietzsche reminds us, is the highest will to power ever exercised among human beings. (*Twilight of the Idols*) The highest will to power is an interpretation of existence through the affirmation of life, a positive, loving enhancement of existence, that is, existence is given meaning when it is interpreted. But to affirm life one needs to embrace both the good and the evil of existence. The embracement of good and evil is, according to Nietzsche, the conquering of the ascetic ideal, yet not without it being primarily useful and a necessary stage in the spiritual preparation of humanity for overhumanity: one has to have been a Christian to become an anti-Christian. The ascetic ideal being bent inward by the ascetic priest needs bending outward to liberate the imprisoned will from living in the present and past alone to living in the future, by willing the past to return from the future to the present. The will eternally willing itself by willing the past to return to the present experiences the entirety of time in the present moment. Such living in the wholeness of time is, according to Nietzsche, the capacity of the Overman alone. Existing in the wholeness of time is found in Christ's being the Alpha and Omega, the beginning and the end, the uniting of both ends at the junction of two infinite circular lines of existence and time in every present, eternal moment, which Nietzsche suggests in "On the Vision and the Riddle" (TSZ), where Zarathustra, arguing with the dwarf about the time, communicates his idea of the eternal return. Zarathustra's mind is weighed down with the heaviest thought that the path of existence is infinite in both directions, the future and the past, and crooked, that it circles upon itself.

In this regard, Nietzsche's conception of the eternal return may be considered in light of Christ's unconditional love of humanity, to which attests Christ's incapacity for physical resistance and, one may add, free death, in *The Antichrist*, and Christ's never renouncing his faithful love of humankind in the face of corporeal death. Christ's love can be interpreted by the will to power as interpretation, to be the highest will to power, according to Nietzsche. This interpretation is at once not only an interpretation but also a confirmation of the will to power as interpretation. (BGE # 36) In order to have and exercise such power, Christ had necessarily to affirm his life and life in general, and he did so because he simply embraced spiritual good and evil, saying that there will always be the (spiritually and materially) poor and the (spiritually and materially) rich, there will always be good and evil in the world, but it is incumbent on human beings to accept them properly in order to conquer them; likewise one only needs to die spiritually to conquer spiritual and physical death. This is the sure way of the Son of Man, as Christ called himself, to become what he actually is, to become himself: the Son of Man is taken to mean nothing other than Man giving birth to his Son, who is the Overman in Nietzsche's language. But the aforementioned embracement of good and evil by Christ must stem from his having already conquered the ascetic ideal in the eternal return as discussed above.

The question of how Christ managed to conquer his ascetic ideal must be raised on the basis of this ideal. Christ conquered this ideal through spirituality, having the highest will to power. The origin of Christ's highest will to power is his incapacity for physical resistance against others. His incapacity for resistance against his enemies paradoxically stems from his absolute control over his own (animal) instincts. Christ's control over his instincts is a sheer indication of his having overcome them. The overcoming of his instincts is what I call the bending outward of his bent-inward ascetic ideal by discharging them. Christ's discharge of his instincts took the form of self-reflexive spirituality, in Nietzsche's formula: the body feeds the spirit. The spirituality of Christ liberated him from the oppressiveness of his instincts and enabled him to reach such a state of mind as to live in the present (applicable to animals alone), in the past (the case with human beings who suffer from the imprisonment of their will), and in the future (the capacity of the Overhuman), which made Christ at once human and divine, the Alpha and the Omega, the beginning and the end, the circular return of existence unto itself, the highest affirmation of life through love on earth, the first and last philosopher of all time.

## Conclusion

Examination of the Golden Rule finds Nietzsche's philosophy deeply rooted in Christianity while Christianity, when placed in the context of Nietzsche's idea of the eternal return, finds its image of an Overman in the self-reflexive mirror of Nietzsche's philosophy.

The ascetic ideal is linked with creativity. The bent-inward ascetic ideal feeds the bent-outward one; that is, suffering feeds creativity. When creativity is performed and feels satisfied, the bent-outward ascetic ideal turns inward again, and suffering resumes. Suffering again accumulates to the point of bursting, getting discharged from the internal outward into the external through creativity.

The above-described processes never end with spiritual, creative human beings in the eternal return of good and evil, for good eternally seeks to affirm evil. Affirmation of evil through good is connected with the human perception of time. Time as a never-ending circle liberates the human will from the past within its circular freedom. Circular freedom provides means to re-establish harmony with the world at every moment of human existence. Christ was capable of such a harmonious reconciliation with the world at every moment of his life on earth through spiritual creativity in heaven.

## Bibliography

*The Holy Bible* New King James Version, Hagerstown: Thomas Nelson, Inc., 1990.

Nietzsche, Friedrich. *Thus Spoke Zarathustra, The Antichrist, Twilight of the Idols* and *Beyond Good and Evil* in *The Portable Nietzsche*, tr. Walter Kaufmann, New York: The Viking Press, 1954.

— *On the Genealogy of Morals* in *On the Genealogy of Morals* and *Ecce Homo*, tr. Walter Kaufmann and R.J. Hollingdale, New York: Vintage Books, Inc., 1989.

— *The Gay Science*, tr. Walter Kaufmann, New York: Vintage Books, 1974.

— *The Gay Science* tr. Walter Kaufmann, New York: Random House, 1974.

Loeb, Paul S "Finding the Übermensch in Nietzsche's *Genealogy of Morals.*" *Journal of Nietzsche Studies* (#30, 2005): 70 – 101.

www.ingramcontent.com/pod-product-compliance
Lightning Source LLC
Chambersburg PA
CBHW071306040426
**42444CB00009B/1891**